W9-BJK-067

DISCOVERING U.S. HISTORY

RevolutionaryAmerica

1764–1789

DISCOVERING U.S. HISTORY

The New World: Prehistory–1542

Colonial America: 1543–1763

Revolutionary America: 1764–1789

Early National America: 1790–1850

The Civil War Era: 1851–1865

The New South and the Old West: 1866–1890

The Gilded Age and Progressivism: 1891–1913

World War I and the Roaring Twenties: 1914–1928

The Great Depression: 1929–1938

World War II: 1939–1945

The Cold War and Postwar America: 1946–1963

Modern America: 1964–Present

DISCOVERING U.S. HISTORY

Revolutionary America
1764–1789

Tim McNeese

Consulting Editor: Richard Jensen, Ph.D.

CHELSEA HOUSE
PUBLISHERS
An imprint of Infobase Publishing

REVOLUTIONARY AMERICA 1764–1789

Copyright © 2010 by Infobase Publishing

Chelsea House
An imprint of Infobase Publishing
132 West 31st Street
New York NY 10001

Library of Congress Cataloging-in-Publication Data
McNeese, Tim.
  Revolutionary America, 1764–1789 / written by Tim McNeese.
    p. cm. — (Discovering U.S. history)
  Includes bibliographical references and index.
  ISBN 978-1-60413-350-9 (hardcover : acid-free paper) 1. United States—History—Revolution, 1775–
1783—Juvenile literature. 2. United States—History—Revolution, 1775–1783—Causes—Juvenile literature.
3. United States—History—Confederation, 1783–1789—Juvenile literature. I. Title. II. Series.

  E208.M398 2009
  973.3—dc22

                              2008055179

Chelsea House books are available at special discounts when purchased in
bulk quantities for businesses, associations, institutions, or sales promotions.
Please call our Special Sales Department in New York at (212) 967-8800
or (800) 322-8755.

You can find Chelsea House on the World Wide Web at http://www.chelseahouse.com

The Discovering U.S. History series was produced for Chelsea House
by Bender Richardson White, Uxbridge, UK

Editors: Lionel Bender and Susan Malyan
Designer and Picture Researcher: Ben White
Production: Kim Richardson
Maps and graphics: Stefan Chabluk
Cover printed by Bang Printing, Brainerd, MN
Book printed and bound by Bang Printing, Brainerd, MN
Date printed: April 2010
Printed in the United States of America

10 9 8 7 6 5 4 3 2 1

This book is printed on acid-free paper.

All links and web addresses were checked and verified to be correct at the time of publication. Because of
the dynamic nature of the web, some addresses and links may have changed since publication and may no
longer be valid.

Contents

Introduction

The Boston Massacre

On the morning of February 22, 1770, protesters gathered outside the home of Ebenezer Richardson in colonial Boston's North End. Richardson had been identified as an informant for the local British customs inspectors, officials who were increasingly disliked by people living in the British colonies. That Richardson had informed for the despised customs agents made him, in the minds of many patriotic Bostonians, a target.

The mob had the Richardson family pinned inside their house as they tossed garbage, sticks, and rocks. Mrs. Richardson was hit by a rock and her two daughters were nearly hit as well. An angry Ebenezer Richardson showed his face in an upstairs window. As the mob continued to toss items at his house, Richardson loaded his musket with bird shot and fired at the mob. The pellets peppered several people, including a boy named Christopher Seider [some believe his name was Snider], who took eleven pellets in his chest and stomach. The boy died that night.

After the frustrated Richardson fired his shot, the mob rushed the house and surrounded him. He was spared his life and was charged with murder.

On February 26, Christopher Seider received, according to historian Allen Weinstein, "the best-attended funeral yet held in America." Thousands of Bostonians joined the funeral procession, walking down the city's snow-lined stone streets. The funeral was an orchestrated Patriot event, all choreographed by one of the city's loudest protesters, Samuel Adams, the leader of the Patriot group known as the Sons of Liberty. Adams placed a large group of boys at the front of the procession, ahead of the coffin. Almost none of those marching or even attending the funeral had known Christopher before his death. But he had become a martyr for the Patriot cause, a youthful symbol of protest against British authority.

AN ANGRY CITY

For nearly two years prior to this tragic incident Massachusetts residents, including those in Boston, had struggled against the royal government of their colony. Governor Francis Bernard had called for red-coated, British troops to be sent to Boston from Canada to discourage mob protests. In October 1768 the first redcoats arrived by ship, the 14th and 29th Regiments, numbering as many as 1,000 soldiers. These troops, some of whom had fought against the French during the French and Indian War (1755–1760), were not wanted in the colony.

Antagonism spread between soldiers and Patriots. The troops may have been in control of their street-corner sentry posts, where they sometimes harassed locals, but the Patriots told the merchants what to do. Angry, frustrated citizens began prowling the streets at night. The soldiers were a constant reminder to the Patriots that the townspeople were not in charge of their own community.

The Sons of Liberty worked hard to push the antagonism between redcoats and Boston citizens to the edge. In 1769 Samuel Adams, the group's recognized leader, wrote of the Loyalists (those who continued to support the British), according to historian Allen Weinstein: "There is a cursed cabal [group of plotters], principally residing in this town who were perpetually intriguing to bring about another parliamentary tax act; for no other purpose than that they might feast and fatten themselves upon the spoils and plunder of the people." Adams even tried to enflame public opinion against the redcoats by suggesting that the British "in calling for a military force under pretence of supporting civil authority, secretly intended to introduce a general massacre." To some people, the death of Christopher Seider appeared to support Adams's excited claim. During the days following the boy's funeral, the seething anger of the people of Boston expressed itself as never before.

CLASH IN THE STREETS

On March 2, 1770, just four days after the funeral, an off-duty British redcoat named Thomas Walker went to a Boston "ropewalk" (a long narrow building where rope is made) looking for a part-time job to supplement his meager wages as a soldier. Walker was not only turned down, but the factory's owner, William Green, mocked him. Before long other workers were joining in the fight, giving Walker a beating. Walker returned later with a group of his fellow soldiers. Another fight broke out, with the redcoats breaking it off and leaving. The next day, March 3, three soldiers returned and started another fight. Again, the redcoats received the worst of it, with one suffering a fractured skull. The following day was Sunday and no additional violence took place in the town.

A tense Monday, March 5, found snow on the ground a foot deep. Trouble was about to explode again in the streets of Boston. On King Street, near the hated British Custom House and the Main Guard, the headquarters for British troops, yet another fight had broken out. This one was between a colonial, Edward Gerrish, and a British soldier.

The fighting brought other Bostonians to the snow-covered street. Within a few minutes a redcoat sentry named Private Hugh White was surrounded by as many as 50 angry citizens, with most taunting him to fight. The nervous private loaded his musket, then ran down the street to the steps of the Custom House, fixed his bayonet, and turned toward the shouting mob. That mob was out of control, angrily venting at the lone soldier as they pelted White with snowballs and large pieces of ice. Some in the crowd shouted they wanted to kill the soldier. The town watchman arrived and begged the crowd to stop, assuring White there was no need for further violence. White shouted for the Main Guard to come to his rescue. Fellow redcoats soon appeared.

The animosity that evening spread like a contagion. Other mobs gathered on other street corners within blocks of King Street, shouting at other redcoats. Soldiers brandished guns, bayonets, and clubs. Some officers shouted for their men to remain calm. The British officer whom Gerrish had originally insulted ordered his men to return to their barracks before something unfortunate happened. To draw more citizens into the fray, some mob participants shouted "Fire!" Church bells were soon clanging, calling out volunteer firefighters. Several streets in Boston were descending into an edgy, angry chaos.

Over on King Street, the mob grew, as men, women, and boys descended on Private White's sentry box. Their number soon swelled to 300 or 400. The Main Guard joined White, led by Captain Thomas Preston. Captain Preston had not shown up to confront the mob. To do so would have been sheer folly. Instead, he had planned on escorting Private White to safety. However, so many Bostonians surrounded the soldiers, they were unable to cut their way through the throng. Keeping his cool, Preston ordered his men to move back toward the Custom House where they formed an arcing line, trying to keep anyone from getting behind them. More people showed up, ready to fight fires, in answer to the church bells, which were still tolling loudly. Preston shouted for the mob to disperse, but emotions were controlling the scene. The crowd cried out for the soldiers to fire at them.

Then, a brave city official, a justice of the peace named James Murray, arrived to read a copy of the Riot Act. The reading of this law during a mob action was required before the law was considered in effect. As Murray approached, the crowd knew his intent and knew that, if they managed to provoke the soldiers to fire on them, the redcoats would be on shaky legal grounds. The crowd then turned on Judge Murray, who was sent running from the scene before making his reading. Men brandishing clubs struck the soldiers' musket barrels. Some Patriot organizers on the scene shouted at Preston, taunting him and asking him repeatedly if he intended to order his men to fire. Each time, the exasperated captain answered he did not.

THE FINAL SPARK

Only a foot or two separated the soldiers and citizens. Suddenly, someone tossed a club and struck Private Hugh Montgomery, who lost his balance, slipped on the icy street, and dropped his musket. The soldier then rose to his feet, having retrieved his gun, lowered it toward the crowd and did just as the mob had been imploring the redcoats—he fired.

Seconds must have seemed like minutes at that moment. Following Private Montgomery's shot, the other troops fired

Following a 1773 British tax on locally produced tea, "A Society of Patriotic Ladies" in North Carolina meet to sign a protest agreement not to drink tea and not to allow British goods to be sold in the colonies.

as well. They had not received orders from Preston. The crowd advanced despite the shots, but few got close enough to club a redcoat. The soldiers reloaded, and fired again, not all at once, but over a period of minutes. Some in the crowd fell, as the larger mob began to scatter. Some returned only to pick up the wounded. The soldiers then fired a third round. By this time, a stunned Captain Preston had regained his senses, and began striking downward the musket barrels of his men. Historian Weinstein notes Preston's anguished orders: "Stop firing! Do not fire!" Preston's men began claiming they thought he had ordered them to shoot. The captain ordered his men to return to the Main Guard, where they were placed in formation, awaiting the return of the angry mob of citizens.

Back at the Custom House, shocked Bostonians looked along King Street at the blood stains in the snow. Five civilians lay dead or dying: a free black named Crispus Attucks, an Irish Catholic immigrant, an apprentice sailor, a local 17-year-old, and the son of the owner of the ropewalk where earlier violence had led to this singular event.

For several years, angry colonials had cried out against decisions made by King and Parliament. Protests had become commonplace from Boston to Savannah, Georgia. Increasing numbers of English subjects, who had in earlier years accepted without question the authority of the Crown over their lives, were striking out against any and all representatives of British power. For nearly 175 years, the British had held sway over the 13 colonies that hugged the Atlantic Coast of North America. But that grip was loosening. Why were so many colonials so dissatisfied? What were they angry about? Where would it all lead? What did the future hold for those who were refusing to think of themselves as Englishmen and women, but were ready to give themselves a new identity—that of Americans?

Revolutionary America: 1764–1789

By 1789, when the U.S. Constitution had been ratified and George Washington had been made the first president, the United States did not fill even half of its present area. Most of the land west of the Mississippi River belonged to Spain. The 13 colonies had become states and the frontier lands were territories.

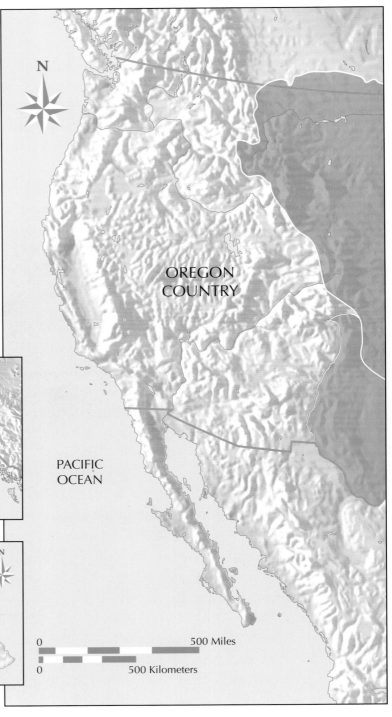

OREGON COUNTRY

PACIFIC OCEAN

N

0   500 Miles

0   500 Kilometers

ALASKA

N

0   500 Miles

0   500 Kilometers

HAWAIIAN ISLANDS

N

0   500 Miles

0   500 Kilometers

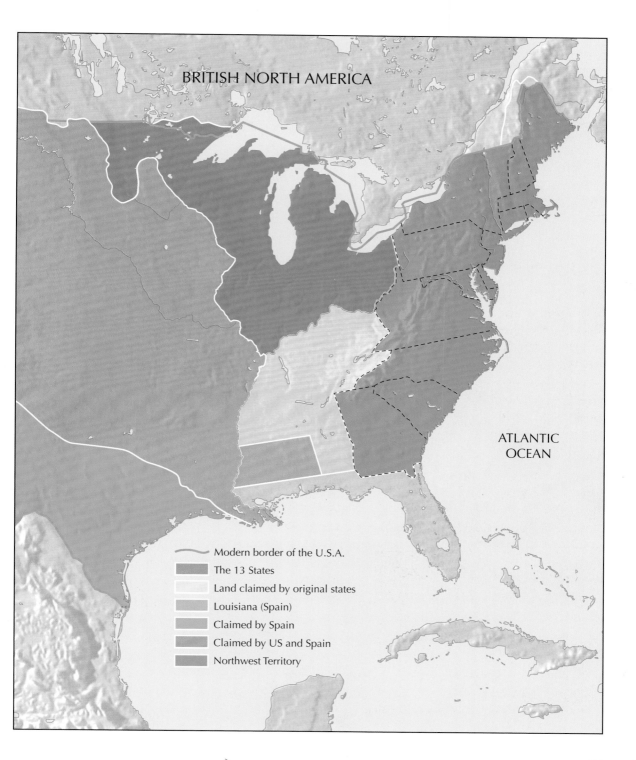

BRITISH NORTH AMERICA

ATLANTIC
OCEAN

Modern border of the U.S.A.
The 13 States
Land claimed by original states
Louisiana (Spain)
Claimed by Spain
Claimed by US and Spain
Northwest Territory

1

From War to Protest

The conclusion of the French and Indian War (1755–1760) brought significant change to the balance of power in North America. The war ended with the French defeated and removed from New France (today's Canada). The British, who had established the 13 colonies during the 1600s and early 1700s, suddenly found themselves with a vast amount of territory, including Canada and stretching south to Florida and west to the Mississippi River. Since the war had begun over control of the Ohio River Valley, the English colonists in America believed they were now free to move west into that region. But that expectation did not pan out immediately.

PROCLAMATION LINE OF 1763

While the French might have been out, the American Indians of the Ohio Country were not. The British occupied former French forts in the region, but they did not continue the same even-handed relations with the Indians. This led to various Indian rebellions, mostly led by the Ottawan Chief Pontiac, but the British quelled these by force or treaties.

To take away future antagonism between the British and the Indians of the Ohio Country, the Crown passed the Proclamation of 1763, which declared the lands west of the Appalachian Mountains closed to future emigration. King George III, who had just come to the throne in 1760, stated: "It is just and reasonable and essential to our interest and the security of our colonies that the several nations or tribes of Indians with whom we are connected, and who live under our protection should not be molested or disturbed." While this may have pleased the Indians, it did not satisfy the colonists. Many British colonials had supported the French and Indian War because they thought it would open the region to occupation. Now those lands had been set aside as a vast Indian reserve. Feeling the British had no means to back up their proclamation, many colonists chose to violate the Crown's order and moved west anyway, even at the risk of being killed by Indians. This defiance of British authority was one of the first bricks in the wall of colonial opposition to the Crown.

A STAGGERING DEBT

The British had won their war with the French and gained a vast North American empire—but at a huge price. Thousands of troops, scores of warships, and millions of pounds of equipment, weapons, food, and supplies had been shipped across the Atlantic. The occupation of the western forts and the takeover of Canada represented additional expenses. The result was that Great Britain emerged from the war with its national debt almost doubled: the debt had been 73 million pounds in 1755 and was a staggering 137 million pounds by 1760. Such amounts were equivalent to tens of billions of dollars today. Some leaders in London began to talk of their country going bankrupt. The debt could not ride forever. It had to be paid somehow. But how?

By the early 1760s British authorities believed they had hit upon the answer. The 13 colonies had certainly gained by the war. They were no longer menaced by the French to the north. The Indians were being monitored by British forces stationed in the western forts, an ongoing cost to the Crown. Logic, reason, and economic necessity made one thing clear to the authorities: The colonies would have to be taxed and soon to help pay for a victory that had improved their lives more than those of anyone else in the British Empire. It was not fair to make the people living in the British Isles pay the full bill for protecting the colonists—and besides, they already paid 30 times more in taxes than their American counterparts.

Prior to the war the British Crown had not taken an active interest in its colonies in North America. It did not order the lives of the colonists or place financial burdens on them through taxation. But the war changed that. The Crown believed the colonies owed something to the Mother Country for protecting them against the French.

EARLY TAXATION

In April 1763 a new prime minister and chancellor of the exchequer rose to power to serve George III and the British people. His name was George Grenville, a 50-year-old member of Parliament. (As chancellor of the exchequer, Grenville headed the treasury.) Grenville was immediately given the responsibility of dismantling the giant British war machine that had fought the French and Indian War in the colonies, as well as its European counterpart that had fought a parallel conflict known as the Seven Years' War. Soon, the number of active British troops was reduced everywhere except in the

American colonies. There Grenville doubled the number of soldiers to 7,500 men. He felt this was necessary to provide future defense of the colonies. This move became immediately controversial among British subjects in America.

While such military forces had been dispatched to fight the French, they had also been used already to fight American smuggling. During the 1600s and early 1700s, the Crown had established a series of navigation acts on the colonies in an effort to regulate trade. The result had been that the colonists ignored such acts, refusing to pay customs duties, and instead smuggled in goods behind the backs of British authorities. With so many troops in the colonies because of the war, British ships could patrol American waters to search for smugglers. It became usual for soldiers, armed with writs of assistance (special permissions issued by the king), to enter colonial businesses and homes to search for smuggled goods. In 1760 Boston merchants had hired a lawyer named James Otis to challenge the legality of such writs. He had failed in his case, and the aggravating searches continued, further angering colonials. The smuggling did not stop.

Now, Lord Grenville was prepared to place new taxes on the colonies. He did not seriously consider whether Parliament had the authority to tax the colonists. They were British subjects, Englishmen and women who were represented in Parliament, even if no colonists had voted for anyone in Parliament. Grenville's view, held by many British officials, was that the colonies were "virtually" represented by the British government in London. Defining the "consent of the people" quite loosely, Grenville thought the Crown, which included Parliament, could legislate over the colonies legitimately. Parliament had, of course, passed laws that applied to the colonies for many years. So, why not now?

However, some colonists disagreed. They believed in actual representation. Almost since the establishment of the first British colony in North America, the colonists had demanded they be allowed to physically vote for their representatives. This had become the standard practice in America: Colonists in all 13 colonies regularly elected their legislative leaders. Thus, the history of the colonies had never been based on virtual representation, but rather on actual representation.

Armed with his theory of representation, Lord Grenville went forward with his plans to tax the colonies. In the spring of 1764, the prime minister convinced Parliament to pass the Revenue Act. Commonly known as the Sugar Act, it revised old import duties and created new ones on a package of trade goods the colonies commonly imported, including sugar, molasses, wines, coffee, and indigo, the latter producing a valuable purple dye. The act also barred the importation of French wines and foreign rums, requiring the colonies to purchase such items direct from British exporters. At the heart of this act was Grenville's intention to keep the colonists from buying sugar from the French West Indies, and to prevent them from bypassing British traders. In addition, the Sugar Act called for British customs vessels to patrol colonial waters and look for smugglers. It also established a vice-admiralty court in the Canadian province of Nova Scotia, where captured American smugglers could be tried, rather than in the colonies.

Smuggling was a lucrative business for American shippers and merchants. The practice allowed colonists to import and sell a wide variety of trade goods without the expense of regulation by British customs laws. Grenville believed the customs service was losing 700,000 pounds of income annually due to colonial smuggling.

The Sugar Act raised an immediate howl of protest from American shippers, merchants, and consumers alike. It was clear that Grenville's act was intended to raise tax revenues

Bostonians protesting the Stamp Act burn the stamps in a bonfire. From 1765, colonists had to pay a tax on printed items. A stamp was put on each item as the tax was paid in shillings and pence.

in the colonies. Americans saw this as a direct break from tradition. Early acts of Parliament—such as the Navigation Acts of the 1660s and the Molasses Act of 1733—had tried to restrict the amount of trade colonists could engage in with foreign traders and shippers. The Sugar Act was different. It had been established to raise money for the overdrawn British treasury.

As colonial subjects, however, and with the Crown so far away in England, what could be done? Colonial protests against the Sugar Act generally received little response. In 1764, 8 of the 13 colonial legislatures sent petitions to Parliament calling for the repeal of the act. Parliament, Grenville, and King George III were not deterred. The act remained. Another form of protest was organized. On May 24, 1764, at a Boston town meeting, citizens pledged to boycott English imported goods. They hoped this might put economic pressure on Great Britain to abolish the Sugar Act.

Another Grenville Act passed in 1764 put another form of restriction on the colonies. With the prime minister's encouragement, Parliament passed the Currency Act, which outlawed colonial issues of paper money. The act, in part, was well-intended, since the colonies were facing post-war economic difficulties, brought in partially by the overprinting of paper currency. However, it made doing business more difficult, since there was little hard currency (gold and silver coins) in circulation. It also placed the power of taxation and customs in the colonies into the hands of royal officials, not the legislatures or the people directly.

THE STAMP ACT

The next step in Grenville's campaign of greater taxation and economic domination over the colonies was the Stamp Act, passed in Parliament in 1765. It was patterned after an existing law that had been in place in England for nearly a century. The act effectively created a tax on all paper products and printed materials. It required a royal tax stamp be affixed to everything from newspapers to land deeds to wills to pamphlets to tavern licenses to playing cards—even to paper dice. To make matters worse, the act required the stamps to be paid for with hard currency, gold or silver coins, not paper money.

To counter any potential colonial protest, Grenville called for any revenues raised by the act to be used to pay for British troops stationed in the colonies. The act passed on March 22, 1765, and was scheduled to go into effect on November 1. By the time the colonists received word of the act, they had six months to decide how to protest it. The main objection was not the amount of the tax, but the legal principle in question. The colonists said that they had not given consent for such taxes. A phrase became common on the streets and in legislative halls: "No taxation without representation."

VIOLENT PROTESTS

There were other forms of protest. Colonists formed groups, such as Samuel Adams's Sons of Liberty in Boston, whose aim was to harass officials, especially designated royal stamp agents, and prevent them from selling the tax stamps.

Before establishing the Sons of Liberty, Adams had been a member of the Loyal Nine, a group of Boston artisans, craftsmen, shopkeepers. and a printer. The group organized a street-level protest of the Stamp Act in August 1765. On the morning of August 14, a group of protesters gathered in the streets, where mob members hung a dummy of Andrew Oliver, the designated royal stamp distributor, from a tree on Boston Common. (The practice is called "hanging in effigy.") That night, people went to his house and built a bonfire outside. They shouted insults and some tossed rocks through his windows. Then, they burned the effigy that had been

ISAAC BARRE AND THE SONS OF LIBERTY

The Stamp Act of 1765 drew the immediate ire of many colonials, who viewed it as an attempt to raise revenue rather than regulate trade. The protests that followed included irate pamphlets, articles and cartoons in newspapers, an economic boycott, legislative petitions, and various street demonstrations.

Among the mob actions that took place, none were as loud and angry as those in Boston. The group responsible was formed by Samuel Adams, who was destined to become one of the leading Patriots against British authority. He and his fellow artisans and craftsmen (Adams had been a brewer) formed a resistance group called the Loyal Nine that rallied street demonstrations against designated stamp agents, such as Andrew Oliver.

As word of such demonstrations reached the halls of Parliament, various members spoke out in response. One was Colonel Isaac Barre, a parliamentary liberal, who had opposed the Stamp Act in the first place. During the debate over the stamp bill, he had eloquently reminded his fellow parliamentarians that the colonists had created their world for 150 years without much help from the Crown. As to the claim that the colonies owed their protection to the British military, Barre answered, as noted by historian Robert Middlekauff: "They protected by your Arms? They have nobly taken up Arms in your Defence, have Exerted a Valour amidst their constant and Laborious industry for the defence of a Country . . . whose frontier [was] drench'd in blood."

As the colonists rose up in anger against the Stamp Act, Barre expressed his support, referring to such colonists as "these sons of liberty."

Back in Boston, Patriot leader Samuel Adams read about Barre's response in a local newspaper and noted the phrase. Soon he was using it as a name for his resistance organization—the Sons of Liberty. A few years later, a group of Patriot women were to form the Daughters of Liberty.

hung earlier in the day. (The mob had already destroyed a building they thought was going to be used as the stamp tax office. They were wrong—Oliver had intended to rent the building out to various shopkeepers.) Finally, a frightened Oliver came out of his home and announced to the crowd that he would not carry out his duties as the stamp agent for the city. The mob and their sponsor, the Loyal Nine, had, it seems, gained a victory through sheer intimidation and implied violence.

Such protest groups sprang up in other colonies and their methods were copied over and over. Stamp tax agents were intimidated into refusing to perform their official duties. Governors, afraid of mob actions, announced they would not support the Stamp Act. By the fall of 1765, with the November deadline for stamp sales looming, about half the colonies sent delegates to a Stamp Act Congress, with attendees from New York, Massachusetts, Rhode Island, Connecticut, New Jersey, Maryland, and South Carolina. This was an important step in opposition to Great Britain. For the first time since the Albany Plan of Union in 1754, an intercolonial body had met, signifying some cooperation between the colonies.

As the forms of protest stacked up, officials in London felt compelled to take a second look at the Stamp Act. Pressure was already coming to bear in Parliament through London merchants who were suffering under the colonial boycott, which had brought about a 25 percent decline in exports and imports to and from America. By November 1, the day the Stamp Act went into effect, not a single stamp tax agent was willing to distribute his stamps. Its actions having been checkmated by American protests, Parliament had no recourse but to repeal the Stamp Act five months later, in March 1766. The colonists had won a victory in the streets, in the legislative halls, through their writings, and by putting the squeeze on British merchants.

2

The Protest Heats Up

Protesting colonists had gained a win. They had spoken out and demonstrated against the Stamp Act, which they believed to be wrong in both form and theory, and the resulting pressure had forced Parliament to repeal the hated legislation by the spring of 1766. Yet, at the same time the Crown relented and did away with the Stamp Act, members of Parliament passed the Declaratory Act, which affirmed their right and power to place tax legislation over the colonies. One act was gone, but the Crown was not surrendering any of its power.

THE TOWNSHEND DUTIES

Despite the enactment of the Sugar Act and the Stamp Act, neither succeeded in greatly reducing the immense debt Britain had accumulated during the French and Indian War. In August 1766 Lord Grenville was replaced as chancellor of the exchequer by a member of Parliament named Charles

Townshend. (For the moment, William Pitt became the prime minister, although he suffered a mental breakdown before the year's end.) Nicknamed "the Weathercock," Townshend had a reputation as a politician who switched positions and causes according to the prevailing winds. (He was also called "Champagne Charlie" for his wild lifestyle.)

Armed with the Declaratory Act, he soon began pushing for new taxes on the colonies. He directed three major acts, the Townshend Acts, through Parliament. The first of these, the Revenue Act, was designed to accomplish two goals. It placed new duties on common colonial imports, including lead, glass, paint, paper, and tea. While earlier duties had applied to imports into the colonies from foreign countries, these trade taxes were placed on goods being delivered to America directly from Great Britain. The monies raised were earmarked to pay for soldiers assigned to posts in America and for royal colonial officials' salaries. The act also suspended the New York legislature for failing to provide redcoats stationed in that colony with such items as firewood and candles. This move was meant to punish New York for violating the Quartering Act. The result was that New York had only Crown-appointed officials, no elected government.

The Townshend Duties generated immediate protest. There were the usual pamphlets, including one written by a lawyer from Pennsylvania, John Dickinson, titled *Letters from a Farmer in Pennsylvania to Inhabitants of the British Colonies*. It appeared in a series of entries during 1767–1768 in a publication called the *Pennsylvania Chronicle*. These articles were widely read and reprinted throughout the colonies. In his political tract, Dickinson argued that Parliament had the power to regulate colonial trade, but not to wield that power to raise taxes or revenues. He also stated that the dissolving of the New York assembly was unjust and a move against liberty and representative government.

Massachusetts Leads the Way

As with the Stamp Act, colonial legislatures also responded to the Townshend Duties. A confrontation developed in Massachusetts where the legislature drafted a circular letter against the duties, which was then sent to other colonial legislatures for consideration. When British authorities learned of the letter, they ordered it recalled. The Massachusetts legislature voted 92 to 17 to defy that order. In response, in 1768 the colony's royal governor, Francis Bernard, dissolved the Massachusetts assembly. Other governors followed Bernard's example and closed down their colonial assemblies.

A British cartoon of 1766, *The Funeral of Miss Ame-Stamp,* shows members of Parliament crying over the loss of taxes from America while British ships carry unsold goods and stamps from the colonies.

This meant those colonies were governed by men who were not appointed by the people, but by the Crown.

Over the next two years, colonists continued to protest the Townshend Duties. A new organization, the Daughters of Liberty, held public demonstrations during which they worked spinning wheels, making the point that they would make their own cloth rather than import it from England.

JOHN HANCOCK, RELUCTANT PATRIOT

Few men left their mark on the American Revolution with greater flair than John Hancock. No signature is remembered better than the one Hancock penned on the *Declaration of Independence* in the summer of 1776. Yet the Boston merchant joined the Patriot cause later than others.

Born in Braintree, Massachusetts, in 1737, Hancock was the son of a minister, Reverend John Hancock, and Mary Hawke. Growing up in the part of town that later became Quincy, Hancock was friends with another boy who grew up to be a Patriot leader—John Adams. At age five, following the death of his father, John was adopted by his uncle, Thomas Hancock, a successful Boston merchant.

Opportunity came at every turn for John Hancock. He attended Boston Latin School, graduating in 1750. From there, he went to Harvard University and received his bachelor's degree in 1754, while still a teenager. He then went to work with his uncle, learning the ropes of business and shipping, eventually becoming a partner. He lived in England for a year, from 1760–1761, gaining firsthand relationships with his uncle's customers and suppliers. In 1764 Thomas Hancock died and left John everything, including his estate and thriving business. Twenty-seven-year-old John Hancock was one of the wealthiest men in the 13 colonies.

When Britain began passing new duties on imports and exports in America, Hancock did not become too upset. Like most colonial merchants and shippers, John Hancock regularly engaged in

Some colonists pledged to stop drinking tea. Again, the Sons of Liberty organized a boycott, which was not immediately effective. Many merchants had cooperated with the 1765–1766 boycott of the Stamp Act, but in the booming years of 1768–1769 they were less willing, not wanting to interrupt business again. Over time, however, the boycotts had the desired effect. By late 1769 British imports to Boston were

smuggling and rarely paid such duties anyway. When the Stamp Act was passed, he did resist it. The boycott protest that followed was fine with him. He had run out of credit in London at that time and could not buy any more goods. When Hancock told this to the London merchants he normally did business with, they, too, began campaigning against the Stamp Act. In May 1766 one of Hancock's ships brought news of the repeal of the act to Massachusetts.

Meanwhile, the wealthy Hancock was becoming more involved politically. In 1765 he took his uncle's seat as one of Boston's five selectmen. The following year he was elected to the Massachusetts General Court. In 1768 he gained a seat in the Massachusetts House of Representatives. The next year he was elected speaker pro tem (for the time being), even as the dissolved legislature continued to meet secretly and illegally.

Slowly, Hancock became more of a Patriot. Following the Liberty Incident in 1768, he became increasingly outspoken against British authority. When the Revolutionary War began at Lexington and Concord in April 1775, Hancock was a wanted man. The British had marched out of Boston looking for him and Samuel Adams, but had met colonial militiamen along the way. Shots were fired, and the war began.

Hancock became a financier of the war and was elected as president of the Second Continental Congress. During the summer of 1776, when the Congress approved the Declaration of Independence, Hancock was presiding and placed his famous signature on the new document of freedom.

off by 50 percent. In Philadelphia, another bustling American port, trade was down by nearly 70 percent.

THE *LIBERTY* INCIDENT

During the various protests against the Townshend Duties, an incident took place in Boston in the spring of 1768. One of the city's Sons of Liberty was a wealthy merchant named John Hancock. He regularly engaged in trade between New England and the French West Indies, from where he smuggled an estimated 1.5 million gallons of molasses annually. According to historian Harlow Unger, Hancock should have paid 37,000 pounds a year on that amount of molasses, but instead managed to pay a handful of corrupt customs agents only about 2,000 pounds.

On May 9, 1768, Hancock's sloop, *Liberty,* arrived in Boston Harbor loaded with 25 pipes (an amount equal to 3,150 gallons) of Madeira wine. Two inspectors—called tides men—boarded Hancock's ship to identify the cargo and make certain nothing was off-loaded without paying the customs duty. The following day the wine was unloaded, Hancock paid the duty, and nothing out of the ordinary occurred. Within weeks, the *Liberty* took on a cargo of whale oil and tar. Under the existing trade laws, a ship's owner was to post bond for a new cargo before loading it on his vessel, but the practice was that ships were loaded and cleared port, then the bond was paid. Still, Hancock was in technical violation of the law and the chief collector of customs, Joseph Harrison, ordered the *Liberty* seized. (Hancock and Harrison had history. They had clashed before over such procedures and each thought the other arrogant.)

At the same moment Harrison prepared to move against the *Liberty,* another, unrelated incident in Boston Harbor was in the making. Two British warships, *Romney* and *St. Lawrence,* had sailed into the harbor, in need of additional sailors. A common custom of the British navy was to impress men—force them into service against their will—although the practice had been banned in American waters a century earlier. A press gang from the *Romney* had captured an American sailor named Furlong outside a dock tavern. Local citizens came to Furlong's rescue: The press gang returned to the *Romney* beaten and without a "recruit."

In heavy-handed response, the ship's captain ordered the *Romney's* guns aimed at the gathered mob. During this face-off, Harrison requested a boatload of sailors from the *Romney* for assistance in seizing the *Liberty*. As the angry mob watched, the British sailors rowed their longboat to Hancock's ship, lashed the merchant sloop to their vessel, and returned to their ship. Frustrated, the mob took out their anger on Harrison, who was on the dock, along with his son and another customs officer, Benjamin Hallowell. Harrison got away, Hallowell was knocked unconscious, and Harrison's son was dragged off by his hair through the streets of the city. Then, the mob went to the homes of Harrison, Hallowell, and the inspector general of customs, John Williams, where they tossed rocks and broke all their windows.

Quelling the Unrest

Massachusetts royal governor, Francis Bernard, hearing of the incident and anxious to head off greater violence, announced he did not support impressments, then gave the order to custom officials to return the *Liberty* to Hancock, along with his duties. But Hancock refused the governor's offer and demanded his case come before the courts. That case came forward on March 1, 1769, but the Crown chose to drop all charges.

The riots caused by the *Romney's* press gang, plus the *Liberty* incident, caused British officials in London to conclude that Boston was a hotbed of Patriot fervor. In October 1768 two regiments of redcoats arrived in the city. According to historian James Kirby Martin, a local minister lamented: "Good God! What can be worse to a people who have tasted the sweets of liberty! Things have come to an unhappy crisis, . . . and the moment there is any bloodshed all affection will cease." Soldiers remained in the city until the opening shots of the Revolutionary War seven years later.

By the spring of 1770 Great Britain had a new prime minister, Lord Frederick North. In April 1770 Lord North responded to the events of the previous three years, including the colonial protests against the Townshend Duties and the boycott that was hurting British trade. He saw that the duties were costing, not profiting the Crown and called on Parliament to repeal all of them, except the tax on tea. (Charles Townshend did not live to see any of these protests against his hated trade duties: The same year they were enacted, he contracted typhus and died.)

THE BOSTON MASSACRE

Even as this change in policy was made by Parliament and the majority of the duties repealed, many colonists were not happy. They did not like the tax on tea, and they were not convinced that British policy had actually changed. Just weeks before the repeal of the lion's share of the Townshend Duties, a singular event had taken place in Boston, one that stirred colonists up and down the Atlantic Coast—the Boston Massacre.

When violence erupted between street demonstrators and British troops outside the Boston Custom House on the evening of March 5, 1770, five colonists lost their lives and the city became yet again the chief symbol of anti-British sentiment. The soldiers went on trial for murder, yet they were defended by two unlikely men, both outspoken Patriots—John Adams and Josiah Quincy, Jr.

THE BOSTON MASSACRE

Redcoats were guarding Boston's Custom House, where British tax money was stored. Colonists harassed the soldiers and the demonstration got out of hand. Five colonists were killed and seven were wounded. Soon after, a Patriot named Paul Revere issued a pamphet that showed the redcoats deliberately shooting the colonists. This fueled the colonists' hatred for the British and helped start the Revolutionary War.

Adams, who would one day be elected the second president of the United States, did not think like his distant cousin, Samuel, who exploited the tragedy by ordering an engraver to produce an illustration of the event that showed innocent Bostonians gunned down by redcoats, their commander raising his sword and giving the order. John Adams argued in court that the soldiers had been placed in an extremely awkward situation. As noted by historian David McCullough in his biography of Adams, the Boston lawyer asked the jury to consider that the soldiers had been pelted with snowballs, oyster shells, sticks, and "every species of rubbish" even as the mob encouraged the redcoats to fire on them. Trying to put emotions aside, Adams added: "Facts are stubborn things and whatever may be our wishes, our inclinations, or the dictums of our passions, they cannot alter the state of facts and evidence." The soldiers had only defended themselves against an angry mob. All but two of the accused were found not guilty, and those two escaped with nothing more than a branding on their thumbs.

Despite the trial's outcome Samuel Adams still milked all the propaganda he could from the tragic event that came to be called the Boston Massacre.

3

The Boston Tea Party

As violent and antagonistic as the Boston Massacre had been, it was followed by a two-year period of calm. The Townshend Duties had been repealed, eliminating the immediate issue between Crown and colonists, and Parliament made no significant moves to raise the concern or ire of Americans.

THE *GASPÉE* INCIDENT

Only one incident stands out during the period between 1770 and 1772. In 1772 a British customs vessel, the *Gaspée*, ran aground off the coast of Rhode Island. The ship was searching for smugglers. Local citizens came out and took control of the ship, forced off its crew, and then set it on fire. (The ship's commander, Lieutenant William Dudingston, was shot in the groin while resisting the boarders.) British officials made halfhearted efforts to bring those involved to justice, but no one was ever arrested for the *Gaspée* Incident.

In spite of the relative calm, many colonists were still upset with British policies toward them. The dissolved colonial legislatures remained dissolved, and the British tax on tea remained. According to historian Axelrod, King George III had insisted "there must always be one tax," as a symbol of Parliament's right to tax the colonies. Questions remained about the future relationship between the colonies and the Mother Country. Some Americans were beginning to talk about a complete separation from Great Britain. But most colonists were not ready, in 1772, to consider independence. They were still ready to pledge their loyalty to the king, even as they defied Parliament.

FORCING THE ISSUE

In 1772 Lord North began paying royal governors and judges with monies generated by the Townshend Duties. To make certain everyone in the colonies was aware of this latest slap in the face, Samuel Adams established a new Patriot organization, the Committee of Correspondence. He and two other Patriot leaders, James Otis Jr. and Josiah Quincy Jr., also set out, in a report to the Committee of Correspondence in Boston, three primary rights held by the Americans—the right to life, liberty, and property. (They took their cues from a seventeenth-century English political writer and philosopher, John Locke.) The pamphlet also noted the trio's grievances against British authority, such as paying for royal officials out of colonial duties and being forced to house British soldiers in private homes, and helped to clarify the Patriot causes and motivations.

In time, animosity between Crown and colonials raised its head again. In 1773 the Patriots found a new thorn in their side in the form of the Tea Act. That May, Parliament passed the act as a support for one of the largest monopolistic trading firms in Great Britain, the British East India

Company. The firm was in decline, partly because it was poorly run, partly because of the tea boycott organized by Boston merchant and shipper John Hancock (which had caused the colonial sale of the company's tea to drop from 320,000 pounds [145,000 kilograms] in 1768 to just over 500 lbs [225 kg] in 1773), and partly because of rampant smuggling (which brought Dutch, not British, tea into the colonies).

The Tea Act allowed British customs officials to collect the old Townshend duty on tea (the last of his duties) and then secretly return part of those monies to the British East India Company to help bolster its bottom line. Also, the new tea law gave the company the exclusive right to sell tea in America. It could sell that tea at a lower price, low enough to make it cheaper than smuggled tea which was regularly imported in violation of British trade law. Such tea, of course, was imported without paying the required duty. British officials believed they had killed many birds with one stone. The British East India Company could be saved from bankruptcy. It had a monopoly on selling tea to the colonists. Monies from customs duties would wind up in the pocket of the ailing firm. And smuggling would become useless, since the company's tea imported into the colonies could be sold cheaper than the smuggled variety. (British authorities were intent on passing a Tea Act on the colonies at that time, since London warehouses were stuffed with 17 million pounds of tea, which would likely rot if it could not be sent to and purchased by the colonies.)

THE CALM IS BROKEN

Everyone would win under the new Tea Act passed on May 10, 1773—at least, that's what British officials believed. They believed the Americans would buy the cheaper legal tea over the smuggled kind. But they had miscalculated.

Colonists were not only going to refuse to buy British East India Company tea—they were not even going to allow it to be imported in the first place. The colonial objection to the new Tea Act was not about the amount of the tax. At three pence a pound, the amount was insignificant, and a colonial

HISTORY BETWEEN ADAMS AND HUTCHINSON

Few of the early men who rallied others to the Patriot cause played a greater singular role than Bostonian Samuel Adams. His cousin John Adams, according to historian George Carey, credited him as a key figure in the Revolution: "Without the character of Samuel Adams, the true history of the American Revolution can never be written. For 50 years his pen, his tongue, his activity, were constantly exerted for his country without fee or reward." His was an early voice of opposition to Parliament. In 1748, even before the French and Indian War, Adams had published a weekly newspaper, which aimed, as noted by historian William Wells, to "defend the rights and liberties of mankind." Between 1765 and 1775, the year the Revolutionary War erupted, Adams spoke out against British taxation and growing control over the colonies.

Adams had little appreciation for any British officials, but he despised Thomas Hutchinson, who served first as royal lieutenant governor, then governor of Massachusetts. While Adams's patriotic leanings motivated him against Hutchinson, there was also a personal cause for the dislike.

Hutchinson and Adams's father shared history. Samuel Adams Sr. had been a well-to-do malter—so much so that he was able to send young Samuel to Harvard, hoping he would become a minister (Samuel Sr. himself was a church deacon). In 1740, when his son graduated, Deacon Adams invested in the Massachusetts Land Bank. Its purpose was to provide loans to poorer people by allowing them to use real estate as collateral. The bank allowed payments to be made in paper money, which sometimes proved less valuable than it was supposed to be, since the tea drinker would have to consume a gallon (3.8 liters) of tea every day to end up paying a dollar in tax for one year. It was the principle of the circumstances: Once again, the Americans were expected to pay a customs duty they had never voted to support for the purpose of raising revenue for

colonies often printed more paper money than they had hard currency to back up.

The bank and its practices soon came to the attention of a group of wealthy Massachusetts businessmen, including Thomas Hutchinson, who had served as a member of the General Court. (Older than Samuel Adams Jr. by 11 years, he was also a Harvard graduate.) Elected in 1737, Hutchinson took a strong—and generally unpopular—position against the printing of too much paper currency. Along with several influential friends, Hutchinson convinced the royal governor of Massachusetts to declare the bank illegal and put it out of business. The following year, Parliament upheld the governor's decision, leaving the elder Adams strapped with debts and saddled with lawsuits. He died a few years later.

The younger Samuel Adams never forgave Hutchinson for his role in ruining his father. In 1758, when Hutchinson became lieutenant governor, appointed royally, Adams still bore a grudge. As Hutchinson supported various tax acts enacted by Parliament on the colonies, Adams eagerly rallied his fellow Bostonians against these restrictive laws and defied Hutchinson.

Without question, Adams fought British policy during the 1760s and 1770s because he believed it was restrictive. He also favored a new relationship with Great Britain based on his Patriot political philosophy. How much he was also driven by his dislike of Governor Thomas Hutchinson, historians may only guess. There is little evidence that may be taken from Adams's personal papers. He destroyed most of them in his later years. As for the loyalist Hutchinson, with the approach of the Revolutionary War, he left America in 1774 and spent the remainder of his life in exile in England.

the British Crown. This made the act illegitimate. Historians believe the act may have driven previously moderate American merchants to support the Patriot cause. Hatred of the tea tax was loud and angry. One colonial wrote of the tax and of consuming British East India Company tea: "Do not suffer yourself to sip the accursed, dutied STUFF. For if you do, the devil will immediately enter into you, and you will instantly become a traitor to your country."

The British authorities selected four American cities where the first shipments of the newly taxed tea could be landed—Boston, New York, Philadelphia, and Charleston. Citizens in all four communities were soon up in arms. The Committees of Correspondence leapt into action, as members tried to intimidate designated tea agents in these four ports (just as designated stamp distributors had been harassed several years earlier). In Philadelphia, New York, and Charleston the agents quickly gave in, refusing to carry out their duties. At Philadelphia and New York, ship captains and harbor pilots refused to handle British East India Company tea cargoes, and the tea ships were sent back to London. In Charleston, the tea was off-loaded and placed in a warehouse, where it remained unsold until 1776, when the Continental Congress auctioned it off to help raise funds for the Revolutionary War effort.

THE BOSTON INCIDENT

In Boston, events turned a bit differently. Three East India tea ships arrived in the harbor on November 28—the *Dartmouth*, *Eleanor*, and *Beaver*. Members of the local Committee of Correspondence prevented the tea from being unloaded and insisted the ships return to Great Britain, as they had in other American ports. But the royal governor of Massachusetts, Thomas Hutchinson (whose townhouse had been attacked during the Stamp Act Crisis back in 1765), refused to issue the permits that would have allowed the ships to leave port. A standoff was in the making. According to the customs law, the duty on the tea had to be paid within 20 days of a ship's docking or its cargo was to be seized by customs officials and sold at public auction. Slowly, the days ticked down as the tea ships remained, silently bobbing in the hostile waters of Boston Harbor.

Then, on December 16, the day before the end of the 20 days, Sam Adams held a meeting in Boston's Old South Church. Perhaps as many as 7,000 citizens attended (more than one-third of the city's population). Throughout the day, Adams sent the captain of the *Dartmouth*, Francis Rotch, to Governor Hutchinson to plead for the harbor exit permits that would allow his ship and the other tea vessels to leave Boston Harbor. Hutchinson defiantly refused. By 6 P.M., night was falling, and Adams mounted the Old South Church pulpit and announced: "This meeting can do nothing more to save the country." Gathered Bostonians, on cue, began chanting: "Boston Harbor a teapot tonight! The Mohawks are coming!"

This was a signal to those gathered at the church to move to Boston Harbor, where they witnessed a strange scene. Approximately 150 Patriots appeared, thinly disguised as Mohawk Indians. They were there to carry out a direct act of civil disobedience. As their fellow Bostonians looked on, the "Indians" boarded the tea ships, immediately broke open 342 wooden chests of tea and unceremoniously dumped the 90,000-lb (40,860-kg) cargo into the dark waters of Boston Harbor. The Patriots did no damage to any other property onboard the three tea vessels. When a padlock was accidentally broken, someone later delivered a replacement lock. In all, these organized night raiders destroyed tea worth approximately 10,000 pounds (about $1.7 million in today's money).

A 1784 illustration of the Boston Tea Party of December 16, 1773. Colonists showed their anger at the British authorities' laws by dumping tea from British ships in Boston Harbor.

THE INTOLERABLE ACTS

Within six weeks, word reached London and the ministry of Lord North. Feeling the act of Patriot defiance could not be ignored, the angry prime minister ordered the closing of Boston port. Instead of wasting time and energy ferreting out the culprits who had destroyed the tea, he chose to punish all of Boston: The port was the lifeline of the colonists' economy. North's orders against the harbor were so tight that he allowed only the importation of food and firewood into the city.

Closing the harbor brought a howl of protest across Massachusetts and from other colonies. In Virginia, the fiery Patrick Henry delivered a speech in which he condemned the closing of Boston's port. The following spring Parliament placed more punishments on Boston, through the passage of three acts. The Massachusetts Government Act added powers to the royal governor and banned the holding of all special town meetings across the colony. (The Committees of Correspondence often held such meetings.) The Justice Act provided a trial outside the colonies—called a change of venue—for anyone accused of committing a murder while trying to stop a riot. And the Quartering Act gave more latitude to British military commanders to commandeer private homes and other buildings to house redcoats in the colony.

These acts were intended to force the people of Massachusetts to get in line and bring a halt to all subversive and defiant behaviors. But the colonists were not about to accept what became known as the Coercive Acts or Intolerable Acts. The new laws only served to widen the loyalty gap between the British Crown and American colonists.

4

Collision Course

The relationship between the colonial Patriots and the British Crown was on the verge of a breaking point. Not only did the North ministry and Parliament place the Coercive Acts on Boston, King George III appointed British General Thomas Gage, who had served in the French and Indian War, as the royal governor of Massachusetts and commander in chief of British soldiers in America. The citizens of Massachusetts were placed, in effect, under military rule.

Gage arrived by ship in Boston on May 13, 1774. When he entered the city four days later, amid cold spring rains, he received an equally cold reception from Bostonians. Citizens wore black badges as if in mourning, and church bells across the city tolled as if for a funeral. Undeterred, on June 1 Gage implemented the official closing of Boston Harbor and ordered the capital of Massachusetts be moved from Boston to Salem. In response, the Massachusetts General Assembly, which had already been officially dissolved, began to meet in Salem, calling itself the Provincial Congress. The general and governor ordered this congress to disband, sending a messenger to inform the rebellious representatives. With the courier outside their meeting hall, the delegates held the door closed while voting on a proposal. They called for a Continental Congress, one that would include representatives from all of the 13 colonies.

Later that summer, on June 22, King George III signed a new law designed to limit the power of the colonies. It was called the Quebec Act and it extended the boundaries of the Canadian province of Quebec to include the Ohio Valley and the Illinois Country further west. The act also required that, in these territories, French was to be the language and Catholicism the predominant religion. In one way, George was showing toleration of the French Canadians who still lived in the region the British had gained following the French and Indian War. But the act angered many American colonists, most of whom were Protestant and had always thought the war had ended the possibility of French dominance south of the Great Lakes. The colonists saw the act as yet another by which the Crown did not wish them well.

AN AMERICAN CONGRESS

Desperate and angry colonists agreed to send delegates, or representatives, to an intercolonial meeting to discuss the growing divide between themselves and the Mother Country. In September 1774, 55 delegates representing nearly all the 13 colonies sat down together in a Philadelphia meeting place called Carpenters' Hall as the First Continental Congress. Since most colonial legislatures had been abolished by that time, there was no legal mechanism to appoint these delegates, so the actions they took were entirely illegal. Several important Founding Fathers, remembered today for their support of the American Revolution, were present, including Thomas Jefferson, Patrick Henry, George Washington, John Adams, and his cousin, Samuel.

As they took up their business, these delegates soon focused on several key issues and questions: 1) What were they and their fellow colonists upset about? 2) What did they intend to do about it? and 3) Had the time arrived for the colonies to consider a new relationship with the Mother Country?

The debates on these questions ran in every direction. Almost all the delegates favored the repeal of the Coercive Acts. As to a response, they agreed to petition King George and then organize yet another boycott of British imports from, and American exports to, England. The delegates signed the "Continental Association" on October 20, 1774.

Discussion of a different relationship with Great Britain drew loud argument, however. Conservatives among the delegates called for the colonies to willingly accept the authority of Parliament. Other men suggested that a legal American legislature be established, one that represented the colonies and had the authority and power to make binding laws, while also accepting the scope of Parliament's power. There were also radical voices, such as those of fellow Virginians Thomas Jefferson and Patrick Henry, who argued that the colonies should recognize only the authority of King George and simply ignore Parliament. As for Samuel Adams, he called for independence—a complete break from Great Britain. Few were prepared to accept such a revolutionary position. Nearly everyone in the First Continental Congress, as well as colonists at large, believed it was still possible, in 1774, to work out a new relationship with Great Britain and the Crown, one that would recognize their rights as Englishmen and women. Adams had little choice but to bide his time. In the meantime, the delegates agreed to reconvene on May

10, 1775, if their grievances against the Crown had not been adequately met. They adjourned on October 26, less than a week after agreeing on the "Continental Association."

A WIDENING GAP

Throughout the 1760s and into the 1770s, many colonists experienced a psychological separation from the Mother Country, which played itself out in several ways. Certainly the colonists felt they were being wronged. Parliament, with the king's consent, placed restrictive laws on the colonies, attempting to raise revenue for the Crown through trade laws and customs duties. The British housed thousands of redcoat troops in American cities, which only led to animosity, rebellion, and riot.

Through those years of discontent, many in the colonies were carrying out personal and public practices that indicated the divide between Crown and colonists was widening. For example, by 1774 every colony was holding popularly elected provincial conventions, many in place of their colonial legislatures which had been dissolved by King George. These amounted to unauthorized, but alternative, means providing for some element of representation and voice for the discontented. Royal governors and their appointed councils were losing respect as the colonists listened to them less and less. Militiamen ignored royal muster orders that required them to drill, attending secret drill sessions arranged by local Patriot committees instead. Perhaps most importantly, many colonists were refusing to pay their taxes to British officials. Instead, they paid them to Patriot colonial convention collectors.

PREPARING TO STRIKE

By early 1775 King George III was convinced the American rebellion would never end and that, if something was not done soon to stop it, the effects on the British Empire in North America could be catastrophic. It was the belief of royal advisors and Prime Minister North that if British troops delivered a hammer blow against the Patriot leaders, the growing rebellion would come to an abrupt halt. According to historian Bernard Weisberger, North stated: "Four or five frigates will do the business without any military force." North had no idea how wrong he was.

During the winter of 1774–1775, British officials in England and America prepared their moves against the Patriot cause and its leaders. General-Governor Thomas Gage received orders from London to ferret out and arrest such men as Samuel Adams and John Hancock. George III and Parliament raised monies to pay for additional regular troops to be sent to the colonies, along with three high-ranking British generals, all veterans of foreign conflicts. These three were Sir William Howe, who had even served during the French and Indian War, Henry Clinton, and "Gentleman Johnny" Burgoyne, known for his card playing and womanizing.

As Boston had been the focus of many major Patriot incidents—including the Andrew Oliver Affair, the Boston Massacre, and the Boston Tea Party—British officials declared Massachusetts to be in an official state of rebellion. This special legal designation empowered British redcoats to fire at anyone suspected of being a Patriot. Eventually the British would apply this designation to all of the colonies. For the moment, much of the focus was on Massachusetts.

Searching for Ammunition

In September 1774, just as the First Continental Congress opened its first meetings, General-Governor Gage marched several British soldiers out of Boston into the rural countryside. His objective was to find alleged stockpiles of Patriot weapons, supplies, and ammunition in such small Massa-

John Malcolm, an unpopular Commissioner of Customs at Boston, Massachusetts, is tarred and feathered by colonists in protest against the Intolerable Acts of May 1774.

chusetts communities as Charlestown and Cambridge. When the hated redcoats set out to neighboring towns, as many as 20,000 colonial militiamen went into action to oppose them and protect their military supplies.

With some of those stored munitions hidden away around the Massachusetts community of Concord, the local citizens called a town meeting (such meetings had been made illegal by the Coercive Acts) to raise two companies of Patriot troops. Such volunteers, many of them already colonial militiamen, vowed to make themselves available at a minute's notice if British authorities came into their community, and therefore became known as minutemen. The name was not completely new to the Massachusetts militia, which had used it as early as 1756 during the French and Indian War. According to records, four out of every five men of military age in Concord made such a pledge, signing their names to a document called the Solemn League and Covenant. (Several local single women also signed the document.)

By taking such a pledge, these men and women knew that they were performing an illegal act, that they were agreeing to support the rebel cause, and that they were placing their lives and livelihood in jeopardy. Following Concord's example, citizens in other Massachusetts towns did the same thing. Gage soon understood he had little support outside of Boston and that he was completely dependent on the 3,500 redcoats stationed back in the city.

SECRET ORDERS AND OPEN REBELLION

As 1775 opened, Patriot groups across Massachusetts and elsewhere were busy storing ammunition and muskets. John Hancock had already been appointed as the head of his colony's Committee of Safety, giving him the authority to call out the militia against the British. The Massachusetts Provincial Congress had raised funds for the purchase of additional military supplies, then dissolved its members on December 10, 1774, so that General-Governor Gage could not arrest them en masse.

Gage, meanwhile, continued to regularly dispatch British forces from Boston in search of rebels and their stockpiled weapons. Many times those same redcoat soldiers suffered at the hands of unseen colonial saboteurs. Redcoat boats were found with holes in their bottoms. Redcoat wagons were wrecked and sometimes burned. Piles of straw that had been collected for redcoat bedding caught fire. The British troops' own stockpiles began to disappear from their depot and arsenal sites.

When Gage sent 240 redcoats to Salem on February 25, 1775, where he had received word the rebels were storing cannon and powder, 40 minutemen met them on a drawbridge before the English troops reached the town. The British commander, Colonel Alexander Leslie, ordered the rebel commander, Thomas Pickering, to lower the drawbridge so his redcoats might continue their march, but Pickering refused. With both sides prepared to fire on one another, a local preacher appeared and offered a compromise: Pickering could allow the redcoats to pass, but the English troops could advance only 30 rods (495 feet/150 meters) into Salem, look for the cannon in question, then leave as they had come. Both commanders agreed, and the British, failing to discover the artillery pieces, left. Those cannon, of course, had already been removed to another safe location outside the town. While no shots were fired, such confrontations would continue until an exchange of shots at Lexington, Massachusetts, in April.

Controversial events arose elsewhere. In Virginia a Scottish royal governor, Lord Dunmore, had dissolved the House of Burgesses in May 1774, but the ousted burgesses continued to meet (illegally) in the capital, Williamsburg, at the

Raleigh Tavern. In a speech he delivered on March 23, 1775, just weeks before those opening shots were fired at Lexington, the silver-throated Patrick Henry railed against royal tyranny, as noted by historian Alan Axelrod:

> *There is no retreat but in submission and slavery! Our chains are forged. Their clanking may be heard on the plains of Boston! The war is inevitable—and let it come! I repeat it, sir, let it come!*
>
> *It is in vain, sir, to extenuate the matter. Gentlemen may cry, "Peace! Peace!"—but there is no peace. The war is actually begun! The next gale that sweeps down from the north will bring to our ears the clash of resounding arms! Our brethren are already in the field! Why stand we here idle? What is it that gentlemen wish? What would they have? Is life so dear, or peace so sweet, as to be purchased at the price of chains and slavery? Forbid it, Almighty God! I know not what course others may take, but as for me, give me liberty or give me death!*

ON THE ROAD TO LEXINGTON

Within three weeks of Patrick Henry's impassioned speech in favor of liberty, Massachusetts military governor Thomas Gage received secret instructions from George III's ministers calling for the arrest of the Patriot leaders Samuel Adams and John Hancock. The intent was to end rebellion in Massachusetts altogether. Rumors swirled around Boston that Hancock and Adams were hiding out in the rural town of Concord, a few miles outside Boston. Although Gage had instructions for their capture, he had also been told that British troops were not to fire the first shot in any encounter with colonials. If there was going to be bloodshed, Britain wanted the Patriots to start it. In the meantime, Gage imposed martial law, or military rule, over Boston on April 12.

There were several ways of getting from Boston to Concord, 20 miles (32 kilometers) to the northwest. The route Gage selected required his troops to leave Boston from the north, row across the Charles River to neighboring Charlestown, then follow the road to Concord that passed through other small communities, such as Medford and Lexington. Patriot spies knew of Gage's orders, but were uncertain which road he would order redcoats to take.

A local silversmith named Paul Revere (he did other work as well, including fashioning false teeth) was the head of a ring of citizen spies in Boston. He had recently organized several alarm riders whose instructions were to ride on horseback into the Massachusetts countryside ahead of any advancing British forces to warn of their approach and to call out minutemen. Revere himself had already made a ride to Lexington on Sunday, April 16 to warn Hancock and Adams that Gage was going to send troops to arrest them.

RAISING THE ALARM

On the evening of April 18 several colonial spies, including Revere, were hiding in the shadows of Boston's dark streets waiting for any sign of British troop movement. They knew General Gage had ordered Lieutenant Colonel Francis Smith to lead a force of 700 men to Concord to capture weapons and the two wanted Patriot leaders. Smith would either move to the north end of Boston Neck or he would take the south road to Cambridge and then on to Lexington and Concord.

One alarm rider, a tanner named William Dawes, even pretended to be an intoxicated farmer and staggered past British sentries to get a closer look. Then, he observed what he needed to see. Around 10:30 P.M., British forces under the command of Lieutenant Colonel Francis Smith, including grenadiers and light infantry, were being loaded into whale-boats to cross the river over to Charlestown. He was assisted by a royal marine commander, John Pitcairn.

Earlier that fateful evening, Revere had left instructions to his Patriot comrades to signal to him which way the British were headed out of Boston. They were to place lanterns in the tower belfry of the Old North Church, which faced the Charles River. One lantern in the tower would tell Revere the British were marching out of the south end of the city. Two flickering lanterns meant they were headed north

ARMING THE PATRIOT SOLDIERS

As the war approached, how prepared were Americans for the fight? It might be assumed that many in the colonies owned guns and knew how to use them, but historical evidence for this varies. According to a history study in 2000, a minority of colonial men owned a gun, perhaps as few as one in seven during the 1770s. Another study claims that perhaps 75 percent of men in New England in 1775 owned a gun. Exactly who owned guns is difficult to know.

For those who did own a gun, there were two common types. The fowling piece, which fired small shot, was useful for hunting ducks, turkeys, and small animals, such as squirrels and raccoons. The musket was intended for larger game and for warfare.

The common musket featured a spring-held cock that released a hammer that held a piece of flint. When the hammer struck a metal plate, it caused sparks, which ignited a small amount of gunpowder held in a priming pan. At the priming pan was a tiny touch hole bored into the base of the musket barrel. The small explosion of gunpowder in the pan ignited a larger quantity of powder in the barrel that then sent a lead musket ball out of the barrel and towards its target.

Loading such a weapon involved several complicated steps—placing powder in the priming pan, adding more powder down the gun barrel, toward him and the road to Lexington. Once he saw a pair of lights in the church tower, Revere knew the British were heading north. Revere rode ahead of them, while Dawes took the south road toward Lexington and Concord.

As Revere spurred his horse through that April night, his shouts awakened his fellow Patriots, who hurriedly dressed, grabbed their guns, and headed to Lexington. Revere is often credited with having shouted "The British are coming!" but historian Alan Axelrod notes his actual words were "The

stuffing the one-ounce (28-gram) lead ball down the barrel with a metal ramrod, and then adding a wad of paper to hold the ball in place. The entire process of loading a musket might take between 45 and 90 seconds. Only the most skilled musket users might load and fire the weapon within 30 seconds.

Muskets, with their smoothbore barrels, were notoriously inaccurate. The effective range was short, approximately 50 to 100 yards (45 to 90 meters). There were more accurate weapons available, called rifles. The name came from the grooving, or rifling, of the barrel, which gave the lead ball a tight fit. When fired, the ball spun out of the barrel with greater accuracy and distance.

A well-aimed rifle could be used to hit a small target between 150 and 200 yds (135 to 180 m) away. However, throughout the American Revolutionary War, Patriot forces preferred muskets to rifles. Loading a rifle took twice as long as loading a musket, and while muskets were inaccurate as a single weapon, they were usually fired in unison by a group of soldiers towards targets as close as 50 yds (45 m).

A flintlock musket, powder horn, and shot pouch as used in the Revolutionary War.

regulars are out!" Revere himself reached Lexington within two hours of leaving Charlestown. There he gave the word to Adams and Hancock, then Dawes arrived, and a third rider, Dr. Samuel Prescott. The three men rode on to Concord.

As the hour approached 1 A.M., the three riders were stopped by a British cavalry patrol. While Prescott and Dawes escaped, Revere was captured. According to Axelrod, a defiant Revere announced: "You're too late. I've alarmed the country all the way up. I should have 500 men at Lexington soon." His captors soon turned him over to a Major Mitchell, who cocked his flintlock pistol and placed its muzzle at the alarm rider's head. Calmly, the British officer demanded Revere tell him everything he knew. The anxious silversmith was only too willing, repeating how he had raised many local Massachusetts men who were ready to fight. The British troops soon let him go, however, since they did not know exactly what he had done or what to do with him. According to one version of events, the redcoat cavalrymen kept his horse, and he proceeded on foot. In another, he left them on horseback, disappearing into the early morning darkness.

Revere soon caught up with Adams and Hancock. According to one story, related by historian Allen Weinstein, the militiaman guarding the house where the two Patriot leaders were hiding, Sergeant William Munroe, tried to quiet Revere, telling him he was waking people up with his noise. "Noise!" shouted the excited alarm rider. "You'll have noise enough before long. The regulars are coming out!"

From there, the three Patriots made their way to another Massachusetts hamlet, Burlington. For the moment, the cache of hidden weapons and gunpowder was safe, as were Adams and Hancock. But the British were still headed toward Lexington and Concord, even as minutemen were also making their way, ready to defend the wanted men, their towns, their homes, and the Patriot cause.

5

Separation and War

Through the night of April 18–19, hundreds of British forces marched along a lonely country road toward the town of Concord. At dawn British Major John Pitcairn approached the outskirts of Lexington, his men tired and footsore. Standing on the village green was a group of minutemen who had taken position in a double-line military formation, under the command of Captain John Parker. These Patriot troops agreed they would not let the British pass on to Concord.

The early morning hours were tense in the small Massachusetts town. Townspeople gathered here and there, some in a local church, and others in a drinking establishment, the Buckman Tavern. Still others, to get a better view of what might soon unfold, crouched behind a granite and stone fence to the right of the green where the minutemen were standing. The sound of horse hooves alerted everyone to the arrival of a scout from Cambridge, Thaddeus Bowman.

Breathlessly, Bowman told the minutemen that Parker's men were only a few miles off, and they numbered approximately 1,000. In less than half an hour, they would be there.

Shortly, an advance group of British forces appeared. Some of Parker's men decided the odds were not in their favor and simply walked off. The British commander, Major Pitcairn, faced the 70 or so minutemen before him. He ordered his men into the standard shooting formation, which required two lines of men, with the first line ready to fire a volley shot, then move back behind the second line to reload their single-shot, 14-pound (6.35-kilogram) "Brown Bess" muskets. The second line was to then fire a second volley.

It is here the historical record becomes uncertain. It appears an unidentified party fired his gun, from which side of the skirmish line, no one knows. A British soldier was hit in the leg. A British officer ordered his men to fire a volley into the assembled colonials. Immediately after these shots were fired, Major Pitcairn called for a ceasefire. Gage's orders, after all, were that the British force was not to fire first.

But as Pitcairn shouted his next order, "Form and surround them," his men instead fired a second volley. Why is not clear, but several minutemen, by now scattered about the green, returned fire—not in a volley, but in single shots from several directions. With two volleys fired, the redcoats fixed their bayonets and began charging the colonial militiamen. All of them scattered in retreat, with the exception of Captain Parker, who had been wounded. Remaining on the field, still standing, he tried to reload his musket, but was soon bayoneted by advancing redcoats. As the smoke of the short-lived conflict lifted, the Lexington green revealed eight colonials dead, including Captain Parker. Ten others were wounded. Only one British soldier had been hit in the quick exchange of gunfire that would be remembered as the first fight of the Revolutionary War—the battle of Lexington.

THE FIGHT ON CONCORD BRIDGE

Musket fire split the air that morning on the Lexington green. Colonials had been killed and wounded, but the exchange did not change the redcoats' immediate objective, and they continued on to Concord.

Another Patriot alarm rider, Reuben Brown, rode ahead of the redcoats to give word to the minutemen in Concord. The local commander, Colonel James Barrett, began organizing his men. By 8:30 A.M. the British began to arrive and search various houses for Hancock and Adams, as well as the stored weapons. Finding nothing, the British commander sent a company of men to take control of the South Bridge and seven other men to guard the North Bridge, both spanning the Concord River. Another four companies of redcoats were ordered out to Colonel Barrett's farm.

From his position on a ridge overlooking Concord, Barrett decided not to make any significant move against the British—he knew that thousands of minutemen would soon converge on Concord, and help even the odds. But then Barrett and his 400 militia troops spotted smoke. Concerned the British were burning Concord, Barrett ordered his troops to march toward the occupied town.

To reach the town, the minutemen would have to cross the North Bridge, about a half mile (80 meters) from the main cluster of Concord's dwellings. There, they discovered about 120 British soldiers guarding the span. Even as the Americans moved toward the bridge, the British did not immediately open fire. (Troops on both sides were under orders not to fire first.) But when the minutemen pressed in closer, the British commander, Captain Walter Laurie, moved his men to the opposite side of the bridge.

As the Americans approached, in columns of two, the British lowered their muskets and took aim. Only when the colonials set foot on the bridge itself, did the redcoats open fire. The Americans kept coming, and the British fired off a second volley. Colonials fell as their immediate commander, a Major Buttrick, ordered his men to return fire. Faced with a withering musket barrage, the British quickly abandoned the North Bridge. Three British soldiers had been killed and nine wounded. Yet as the remaining redcoats retreated, the Americans did not pursue them. In fact, only one of them actually crossed the bridge. As he did, a wounded British

This contemporary engraving of the battle of Lexington, fought on April 19, 1775, shows the redcoats, under command of Major Pitcairn, firing at several colonials.

soldier moved, and the colonial shattered his skull with an axe. Such was the nature of the American troops—largely untrained, certainly shy of being professional soldiers.

With thousands of colonial militiamen headed toward Lexington and Concord, the British began a ragged, disorganized retreat to Boston along the same road they had taken so confidently the night before, fired upon along the way by unseen minutemen hiding behind stone walls and trees. The British fought their way through Massachusetts hamlets, sometimes leaving the road to carry out flanking moves so they could attack unsuspecting colonials from behind. Thousands of bullets were fired along the road that would be remembered later as the Bloody Chute, but both sides were using the same inaccurate "Brown Bess" musket, so only one in 300 shots hit their target. Yet, by the time the British staggered into Boston, they had suffered more than 270 casualties—73 dead, 174 wounded, and 26 missing. The shooting war of the American Revolution had finally commenced and the first of a multitude of people were dead.

PURSUING WAR

Lexington and Concord opened a war that would stretch on from 1775 through the last pitched battle at Yorktown in the fall of 1781. Before the conflict was over, it would become a global event that included the French and other European powers.

That spring of 1775, everything seemed centered at Boston. The city was filled with approximately 3,000 British troops, some of whom had been stationed there for years. Now war had opened, and rebellions against threepenny tea taxes were a distant memory. In the aftermath of Lexington and Concord, colonial minutemen surrounded Boston Peninsula with between 16,000 and 20,000 men. However, the Patriots needed artillery.

A British cartoon of Thomas Paine from the 1790s shows him holding a scroll listing some of his works. Pen in one hand and dagger in the other, he carries weapons to overthrow the British monarchy.

Every colonial knew where to find large siege cannon—from the British themselves. A young Philadelphia Patriot named Benedict Arnold, a former apothecary and merchant originally from Connecticut, began a march on British-controlled Fort Ticonderoga. It was situated in northern New York, a fortification bristling with heavy cannon. Other rebels had the same thought, and a group of Vermont Patriots known as the Green Mountain Boys, led by Ethan Allen, moved toward the fort. In May, after joining together, Allen and Arnold moved against the fort and its prized cannon.

THOMAS PAINE

As the Revolutionary War opened, many colonial citizens struggled with giving up their traditional loyalties to the British Crown. But one voice spoke out loudly, in print, against the authority of both Parliament and the king. In 1774, with help from Benjamin Franklin, Thomas Paine had immigrated to Philadelphia from England ready to make a new life. Almost immediately, he was swept up into the fervor of colonial protests. As a serious supporter of republicanism, or government by the people, Paine put pen to paper and wrote some of the most stirring political essays of his time and in modern history.

In early January 1776 Thomas Paine anonymously first published his pamphlet, *Common Sense,* in which he wholly condemned the monarchy while addressing the importance of the American Revolution. His work was extremely popular, selling an astonishing 150,000 copies, more than any previous pamphlet in American history.

Paine's words helped rally Americans through their trying years of conflict with Great Britain. In 1805, more than 20 years following the American Revolution, Founding Father John Adams wrote, according to historian Allen Weinstein: "I know not whether any man in the world has had more influence on [America's] inhabitants or affairs for the past 30 years than Tom Paine."

Allen himself simply approached the main gate of the fort at night and yelled at the sleeping commander, according to historian Bruce Lancaster: "Come out, you old rat!" The fort was immediately surrendered (only 45 officers and enlisted men were inside), and the colonials gained control of scores of cannon.

CAMPAIGN TO CANADA

In short order, Benedict Arnold and his men chose to attack the British in Canada. During the summer of 1775, with Congress's approval, they marched north hoping to drag Quebec into the new conflict. The assault included a two-pronged advance: Colonel Arnold and his men secretly moved through the rugged Maine outback toward Quebec City, while General Richard Montgomery marched his troops into northern New York, along Lake Champlain, with the goal of capturing Montreal.

Both marches went very badly. Arnold's followers became bogged down in Maine, fighting not the British, but the harsh winter weather. Starvation set in—some of the men boiled their moccasins to eat, and others ate their soap. Their boats, fashioned out of green wood, fell apart. Almost half of Arnold's men, 500 out of 1,100, did not complete the trek to Quebec. Montgomery's men did manage to capture Montreal, which was only protected by 150 British regulars. However, Ethan Allen was captured, clapped in irons, and sent to England to stand trial for treason. But British authorities changed their minds and, by October, paroled him in New York City.

Before Arnold advanced on Quebec, he and Montgomery joined forces. During the New Year's Day assault, which took place during a blizzard, Montgomery was killed and Arnold was seriously wounded. By 9 A.M., after five hours of fighting, it was all over. Many of their men were killed or captured. Without the fall of Quebec, the colonials could not expect to hold onto Montreal. Soon, the Canadian campaign was bitterly abandoned, having only managed to drive most of the Indian nations in the region further into the arms of the British.

A CLOSE ORDER FIGHT

During the months immediately following the battles at Lexington and Concord, the Second Continental Congress held meetings to determine the direction of the revolutionary conflict. On June 15 the Congress appointed, unanimously, Virginian George Washington as commander in chief of the Continental army. As a member of the Congress, Washington had made his wishes clear by wearing his old militia uniform from the French and Indian War. Few colonials had more experience as a soldier than Washington. Once appointed, he began making his way to Boston, a trip that would take 12 days. Before he arrived, however, fighting took place between colonial forces ringing the city and the redcoats trapped inside.

General Gage was determined to remove all rebel forces around Boston before cannon arrived from Fort Ticonderoga. He planned to move troops to the south end of the city, capture Dorchester Heights, then march on the rebel center at Cambridge. He set the day of the assault for Sunday, June 18. But when news of his plan leaked out to Patriot leaders, they moved from Cambridge to Charlestown, north of Boston. Here, under the command of Colonel William Prescott, the Patriot militiamen dug in on the 16th, erecting earthen works literally overnight. According to historian Middlekauf, British General William Howe was amazed at the fortifications that now commanded the heights above Boston, noting: "The rebels have done more in one night than my whole army could do in months." From these positions, the militiamen could place cannon and rain shot and shells down on the British ships in Boston's harbor. Gage had no choice but to organize an assault.

By the morning of June 17, Gage woke to discover the rebels well entrenched. The British commander then met with three newly arrived generals—Henry Clinton, William Howe, and John Burgoyne—to plot a course of action. All three generals were highly experienced in war, but jealousy was rife among them, and none had seen combat in more than 10 years. In addition, none had ever commanded large numbers of men in the field, a fact that would prove a problem later in the war.

The generals decided that Gage would order a direct frontal assault up Breed's Hill. They believed that one large-scale battle with the rebels would end the revolution once and for all. They were soon proven wrong. At 3 o'clock on June 17, British troops rowed across the Charles River to the foot of the 130-foot (40-meter) hill. Gage had appointed General Howe to lead the assault. Between 2,000 and 2,500 British redcoats marched up the hill where they met withering rebel fire. After retreating, Howe ordered them up Breed's Hill again, this time stepping over the bodies of their comrades. (Additionally, these British soldiers were carrying 60-lb [27-kg] backpacks and marching through tall grass.) Again, the militia forces poured lead on the advancing columns, who again retreated.

The day seemed lost to the redcoats, but a tenacious Howe ordered a third assault. By now, the colonial forces were running short of ammunition and had no choice but to evacuate their fortifications. Some chose to stay, powder or no powder, and nearly all died of bayonet wounds. But the British had paid dearly for the ground they gained that day. The Americans had inflicted 1,300 casualties, a number equivalent to a 40 percent casualty rate. One hundred

British officers were killed that afternoon, including Royal Marine Major John Pitcairn, who had shouted at the minutemen gathered on Lexington green two months earlier. Among the Americans, the casualties included 100 killed, 271 wounded, and 30 captured. The entire battle had lasted less than one hour.

In the final assault at the battle of Breed's Hill, colonial general Joseph Warren is mortally wounded as the redcoats overrun the American fortifications. From a painting of 1786 by John Trumbull, one of the most famous artists of the Revolutionary War.

A BRITISH STRATEGY

On July 3, weeks following the battle of Breed's Hill (it is sometimes referred to as the battle of Bunker Hill), General Washington arrived in the city. There he discovered a ragtag "army" of undisciplined troops, many of them young farmers, who were living like animals in encampments as filthy as pigsties. As many of the new recruits were unaccustomed to working with muskets, some had accidentally killed their comrades. Sanitation was lacking, and body lice were rife. Washington soon organized this rabble into a working army. He ordered the camps be cleaned up, latrines dug, and discipline restored. The commander from Virginia knew all too well that, if the rebel army was to succeed against professional British troops, they would have to be well-trained. Washington spent the greater part of the next six months whipping his forces into shape.

In November 1775 a colonel in the Continental army, Henry Knox, proposed to General Washington that the heavy cannon at Fort Ticonderoga should be hauled overland to Boston to drive the British out. Washington gave permission, and Knox arrived at the fort in December. Capturing artillery pieces was one thing; transporting them overland and over rivers was another. Knox and his men spent the remaining weeks of 1775 and the early months of 1776 moving their cannon on ox-drawn sleds through the snow all the way to Boston. In all, they delivered 59 pieces, comprising 43 cannon, 14 mortars, and two howitzers.

When the cannon from Fort Ticonderoga began arriving outside Boston in March 1776, General Gage had little choice but to evacuate the city, along with his troops. He worked out a deal with Washington: The American commander would provide the British with safe passage out, while Gage promised not to burn the city. On March 17, 1776, 9,000 British troops boarded 125 ships. Thousands of redcoats abandoned Boston for safety in Halifax, Nova Scotia, along with thousands of Loyalists—colonials with continued loyalty to Great Britain. Bostonians sang Washington's praises. According to historian David McCullough in his book, *1776,* the Massachusetts legislature sent a delegation to congratulate and thank Washington for rescuing their great port city "with so little effusion of blood." Harvard College showed its thanks by giving an honorary degree to Washington, who had little formal schooling.

6

War and Politics

With Gage out of the American picture, the British command fell to General William Howe, who had ordered troops up Breed's Hill. That spring, Howe revealed his strategy for pursuing the war against the rebels. With the Patriot campaigns in Canada having ended miserably, Howe believed the war could be fought completely on American soil. This would allow the British to engage in an entirely offensive war, one in which they could select their objectives as they saw fit. Keenly aware of the presence of many Loyalists in the colonies, Howe noted four particular strongholds of Loyalist sentiment—New York, New Jersey, Pennsylvania, and the frontier backcountry of the Carolinas. By concentrating his war effort in those areas, he could rely on Loyalist support for his troops.

Unfortunately for the British, there were not as many Loyalists as Howe had hoped. When Loyalist forces began campaigning in North Carolina, they made little headway, and were defeated at Moores Creek in February 1776. That summer General Henry Clinton and Admiral Sir Peter Parker attacked Charleston, South Carolina. The British assault was mismanaged (Clinton landed his 3,000 troops in the harbor at high tide, which left many stranded on small islands).

Howe had also anticipated that Loyalists could recruit other colonials to their side, but this rarely took place. As a result, the British began to rely on German mercenaries. These were paid soldiers called Hessians. But these foreign troops committed so many atrocities, including the rapes of several local women, that they turned those colonials who did not earlier support the rebels into the Patriot camp.

DECLARING INDEPENDENCE

While the Second Continental Congress spent much of 1775 searching for direction in the war effort, by the spring of the following year, the issue of independence began to receive serious attention. On May 10, 1776, John Adams presented a resolution to Congress that was designed to clear the way for the colonies to establish constitutional governments based on independence from Great Britain. Five days later the Virginia legislature empowered its delegates in the Continental Congress to propose independence from Great Britain. That resolution was presented by Virginia delegate Richard Henry Lee on June 7 and approved by Congress. The resolution was straightforward in its intent, stating "that these United Colonies are, and of right ought to be, free and independent states, that they are absolved from all allegiance to the British Crown, and that all political connection between them and the State of Great Britain is and ought to be, totally dissolved."

To frame the purposes of the resolution and to explain why the colonies were choosing to free themselves from British rule, a five-man committee was chosen from a cross section of the 13 colonies: John Adams (Massachusetts), Benjamin Franklin (Pennsylvania), Thomas Jefferson (Virginia), Roger Sherman (Connecticut), and Robert Livingston (New York).

This 1797 painting by John Trumbull depicts the five-member committee of colonial leaders presenting the final draft of the Declaration of Independence to Congress in Independence Hall, Philadelphia, on July 4, 1776.

Much of the work of writing the document was done by 32-year-old Jefferson. He was not as well-known as some of his fellow Virginia Patriots, such as Washington and Patrick Henry, but he was highly intelligent, well-read, and a gifted writer. His words were timeless, as his Declaration of Independence reflected the popular sentiments of the Enlightenment: "We hold these truths to be self-evident, that all men are created equal." Jefferson believed that all men were born with rights including those of life, liberty, and the pursuit of happiness. His document included a long list of grievances against King George III. It was a work destined to become one of the most cherished documents in American history.

Jefferson's Declaration of Independence was presented to Congress and a week of debate ensued. On July 1, 1776, the delegates approved Richard Henry Lee's resolution on independence, with nine of the 13 states voting "yea." The following day, three more states accepted his resolution, leaving New York as the single holdout. (Its delegates refused to vote, since they had not received word from their state leaders.) That date, July 2, would be a day to celebrate, John Adams claimed. But two days later, Congress approved the Declaration of Independence, and July 4 became the date remembered since with fireworks and celebration.

THE FIGHT FOR NEW YORK

While political action was taking place in Philadelphia, military action was brewing elsewhere. General Washington moved his forces from Boston to another key port, New York City. The third-largest city in the colonies, behind Philadelphia and Boston, New York boasted an expansive, splendid harbor which could easily anchor a large British fleet. With the Hudson River flowing to the north, the British could also gain a waterway into the American interior. By late June 1776 General William Howe and his troops sailed for the city on ships commanded by Howe's brother, Admiral Richard Howe. The fleet was enormous: 130 ships carrying almost 10,000 British soldiers. Another 150 ships arrived two weeks later with more redcoats and 10,000 Hessians. Still more troops reached New York a month later. By late August General Howe had gathered a force of more than 31,000 men—the largest army Britain would amass during the American Revolutionary War.

Washington prepared to defend the city with 23,000 troops, one of the largest armies he would command. Many of his soldiers were ill, however, and nearly all of them had never seen a full-scale battle. They had recently received the news of the Declaration of Independence, which Washing-

WORDS THAT STIRRED

With the Revolutionary War raging across the colonies during the summer of 1776, the Continental Congress chose to embrace independence and separate from Great Britain. The decision in support of independence was framed in a document written by Thomas Jefferson, of which the opening words are:

When in the Course of human events it becomes necessary for one people to dissolve the political bands which have connected them with another, and to assume among the powers of the earth, the separate and equal station to which the Laws of Nature and of Nature's God entitle them, a decent respect to the opinions of mankind requires that they should declare the causes which impel them to the separation.

We hold these truths to be self-evident, that all men are created equal, that they are endowed by their Creator with certain unalienable Rights, that among these are Life, Liberty, and the pursuit of Happiness. — That to secure these rights, Governments are instituted among Men, deriving their just powers from the consent of the governed.

ton had ordered read to his men. But the greatest fight of their lives lay ahead. The British began to advance on land along the Brooklyn-end of Long Island on the morning of August 22. Among the British commanders present on the field were Henry Clinton, who had been at Breed's Hill, Lord Hugh Percy, who had experienced the nightmare of the Bloody Chute, and General Charles Cornwallis, who had recently been beaten at Charleston. All three were eager and motivated to defeat the rebels.

Almost immediately, Washington's defense line crumbled, in part due to poor coordination between American units. The Americans were outnumbered, outflanked, and outgunned. Washington himself was nearly captured, but

— *That whenever any Form of Government becomes destructive of these ends, it is the Right of the People to alter or to abolish it, and to institute new Government, laying its foundation on such principles and organizing its powers in such form, as to them shall seem most likely to effect their Safety and Happiness. Prudence, indeed, will dictate that Governments long established should not be changed for light and transient causes; and accordingly all experience hath shewn that mankind are more disposed to suffer, while evils are sufferable, than to right themselves by abolishing the forms to which they are accustomed. But when a long train of abuses and usurpations, pursuing invariably the same Object evinces a design to reduce them under absolute Despotism, it is their right, it is their duty, to throw off such Government, and to provide new Guards for their future security.*

— *Such has been the patient sufferance of these Colonies; and such is now the necessity which constrains them to alter their former Systems of Government. The history of the present King of Great Britain is a history of repeated injuries and usurpations, all having in direct object the establishment of an absolute Tyranny over these States.*

when the Howe brothers halted their advance, Washington and many of his men escaped to the southern tip of Manhattan Island. A dense fog and a brewing storm covered their retreat on the night of August 29–30. The next morning, the British and their Hessian allies were stunned that the rebel army had simply vanished.

A Much-Needed Boost

The British did not continue their effective assault for another three weeks, however, as Howe showed an amazing lack of aggression. The delay gave Washington time to organize his next defense, but these were difficult, uncertain days. Morale was low among the Continentals defending the city. Many were sick with dysentery, while others were dying with smallpox. Perhaps one in four of Washington's men was ill.

On September 15 the battle resumed as Admiral Howe sailed his fleet up the Hudson River to land men on the west side of Manhattan, then up the East River where others were positioned on the opposite side of the island. As they had done on Long Island, Washington's advance units shriveled up in the face of superior redcoat numbers. At one point in the fight, as noted by historian David McCullough, a disgusted Washington is said to have thrown down his hat and cried out in frustration: "Are these the men with whom I am to defend America?!" Once again, the Americans barely escaped annihilation.

Only when a mass of men had gathered on the northern end of the island, near where Washington had established his headquarters at Harlem Heights, did the Continentals make a strong stand. On September 16 men under the commands of Henry Knox, old Israel Putnam, and Aaron Burr—a New Yorker who would one day be vice president of the United States—fought hard in a buckwheat field facing the Hudson River, near present-day Barnard College, and beat back Scottish troops of the famed Black Watch Highlanders. It was a singular victory in a string of defeats for Washington in New York City.

Abandoning New York

The British could have ordered masses of men forward to destroy Washington's forces, but once again Howe and his commanders delayed. A month went by without any significant action between the redcoats and rebel army. A massive fire occurred on September 21 on the southern end of Manhattan, which destroyed nearly 500 houses before the British brought it under control. Most of that time the British simply made themselves comfortable, taking residence in the city. On October 12 the British finally attacked again, after landing along the eastern shores of Westchester County, which ended with another rout of Washington's forces. Difficulties abounded for the Continental army's commander in chief when one of his own generals, Charles Lee, refused to send reinforcements from various forts along the Hudson River. (A month later, Lee was captured in a tavern in New Jersey by British dragoons. While a prisoner of the British, Lee proposed a plan he said would bring about a British victory over the Americans. The British turned him down, releasing him in late March 1777. His would-be treason remained a secret for another 70 years.)

By October 16, Washington felt compelled to evacuate Manhattan. But Howe again caught up with him in the village of White Plains in Westchester County, where he defeated the Americans, although his own army sustained twice as many casualties as it inflicted on the rebels. Yet again, Howe did not follow up his field win and crush the American forces. However, after sustaining another defeat in mid-November, including the loss of Fort Washington, Washington soon ordered his men to evacuate New York City. After months of on-again, off-again fighting, he had lost not only the city, but thousands of his men. New Jersey became the new, if temporary home, of Washington's Continental army.

THE TWIN MIRACLES

Washington had not performed masterfully on the various battlefields scattered across New York City, from Long Island to White Plains. At times he had misjudged his enemy and misplaced his forces. That he had not lost his army was due, in part, to General Howe's plodding movements and prolonged delays. Overall, the year 1776 saw only a handful of American victories, among a litany of losses. In some battles the rebels performed well on the field, but were simply outnumbered.

As Washington's weary forces moved into winter quarters over in Pennsylvania, north of Philadelphia—his army had been driven out of New Jersey on December 7 by Hessian troops under the command of British General Charles Cornwallis—many were looking forward to the end of their service enlistments. They had experienced enough, they thought, of military campaigning. The Continental army was ill-housed, ill-clothed, ill-fed, and ill-equipped. Some men were without shoes. They were cold, hungry, dissatisfied, and longing for home.

The Virginia general knew he was facing a crisis of manpower. How could he continue the fight the following spring if he did not have the resources to engage the massive British military war machine now comfortably settled inside New York City? The year had not produced significant wins for him on the battlefield. He and his men needed a victory before the New Year. But how? Where?

Washington searched for a possible British target. Both armies were in winter quarters, and the redcoats would not be expecting a fight with snows falling from New England to Pennsylvania. General Howe had satisfied himself with establishing a string of posts across New Jersey to keep an eye on the Americans. Washington eyed those posts for a possible point of attack. Eventually, he discovered a likely destination—a Hessian outpost across the Delaware River in Trenton, New Jersey.

The Battle of Trenton

Perhaps 2,000 to 3,000 German troops were barracked there and, if Washington could get enough men across the river and surprise the Hessians, he might pull off the victory he so desperately needed. Washington drew up a plan of engagement, a daring stratagem of hit-and-run, perhaps similar to those he had seen during the French and Indian War some 20 years earlier.

Washington's officer staff agreed that an attack needed to be made. On December 22 Colonel Joseph Reed, Washington's adjutant, sent a communication in which he expressed their accord:

> We are all of the opinion my dear general that something must be attempted to revive our expiring credit, give our Cause some degree of reputation & prevent total depreciation of the Continental money which is coming very fast. . . . Even a Failure cannot be more fatal than to remain in our present situation. In short some enterprise must be undertaken in our present Circumstances or we must give up the cause.

The attack must come soon, wrote Reed: "Delay is now equal to a total defeat."

Such an attack would not be easy to accomplish, however. Washington's plan called for three simultaneous crossings of the Delaware River at night in the dead of winter. The attack was scheduled for Christmas morning, when the Germans might least expect any such action. The element of surprise was crucial to Washington's plan. To move thousands of men through the December darkness, cross an icy river, and not be spotted by enemy patrols was unlikely. Nevertheless, Washington pushed forward with his planned attack with the support of his officer staff.

With disaster looming, General George Washington leads his troops in rowing boats across the icy waters of the Delaware River at the battle of Trenton in December 1776, as depicted in an 1851 painting by Emanuel Leutze.

On the night of December 24 the weather proved uncooperative. It was cold, damp, and sleet drenched the men, their horses, and the Durham boats they were to use to cross the icy Delaware River. Yet Washington plunged ahead, knowing the night hinged on a long-shot gamble. The large, flat-bottomed Durhams were brought to their landing sites and filled with men. New England boatmen from Marblehead guided the craft across the river.

The crossing was tense as the barge decks became icy, causing artillery horses to slip. River water and sleet froze to the men's clothing. A few men froze to death. The weather caused hours of delay, and only one of the three planned crossings was actually made. That one was not completed until 3 A.M., and Washington's forces did not take up their march across the dark New Jersey landscape for another hour. The attack would take place later than scheduled, well after sunrise. For a moment, Washington considered canceling the assault, but decided a retreat ran the risk of being discovered as much as an assault. Plus, he determined, the stakes were too high.

As he marched his men nine miles (14.5 kilometers) to Trenton, the weather worsened as snow, rain, and even hail fell on the nearly frozen Patriot army. At Trenton, Washington and his men set up cannon positions—General Knox had managed to get 18 cannon across the Delaware, and among those manning the artillery was a young New Yorker, Alexander Hamilton, who would one day become the first U.S. secretary of the treasury—and opened the assault. The Germans were completely surprised. Their commander, Colonel Johann Rall, had completely disregarded the threat posed by the Americans huddled on the opposite side of the Delaware River. According to historian Bruce Lancaster, the Hessian leader had said: "Let them come. We want no trenches. We will go at them with the bayonet." During the attack that morning, Rall was killed, and more than 1,000 of his mercenaries were captured or killed. The Americans suffered only four wounded. Washington had gained his victory.

Victory at Princeton

A few days later the American commander-in-chief achieved another victory when his men crossed the Delaware River a second time and attacked nearby Princeton. On their way to the small New Jersey town, the Continental army bumped into and fought two British regiments. As his forces threatened to retreat, Washington, mounted on a white horse, rode to the front and personally encouraged his men to fight. With musket balls whizzing past him, Washington rode up and down his front lines. One of his aides was so afraid his commander would be killed, he could not stand to watch and covered his face with his hat. But the charmed Washington did not receive a single scratch, and his men remained on the line until the British retreated. The brave Virginian rode forward, chasing after them on horseback. According to historian Robert Middlekauff, Washington shouted: "It's a fine fox chase, my boys!" The twin miracles of Trenton and Princeton were soon the talk of Patriots up and down the Atlantic Coast.

THE YEAR OF THE HANGMAN

Even Washington knew that his two hard-won victories were more psychological than strategic. His forces went into winter quarters at Morristown, New Jersey, and his army saw little action for the rest of the winter of 1776–1777. These wins were among his last until the end of the war. During the years that followed, he largely engaged in defensive warfare, while trying to keep his army in the field.

Despite these two losses, which the British considered minor, the king's officers felt that 1777 would be the last year of the war. They spoke of the "year of the hangman," seeing the three "7s" in the date as symbols of three hangman's scaffolds. General William Howe, however, remained in New York City until July, then marched his men toward Philadelphia, with plans to capture the city where the Second Continental Congress met. Washington tried to stop him, but was soundly defeated at Brandywine Creek, Pennsylvania, south of Philadelphia (September 11) and at Germantown (October 4), where Washington thought he had pulled off a victory until British troops suddenly surprised him at his rear. Philadelphia fell, as congressmen scattered.

In the meantime, British General Johnny Burgoyne, who was stationed in Montreal, had formulated a plan earlier in the year, one he thought would certainly bring about an ultimate American defeat. It involved a three-prong march toward Albany, New York. As he marched straight south from Canada with his army of 8,000, a second British force was to sail up the Saint Lawrence River, southwest to Lake Ontario. From there, Colonel Barry St. Leger was to march his 1,700 men east along the Mohawk Valley from Fort Oswego to Albany. General William Howe was to advance out of New York City and head north to the same New York destination. If the plan succeeded—and to General Burgoyne, it appeared as simple as a mere matter of marching—the British could cut off the New England states from the rest of the country and bring about the fall of the rebellion.

7

A Shift in Strategy

While General Burgoyne's plan to capture Albany looked brilliant on paper, it did not go well. One leg was never attempted, as Howe chose not to move up the Hudson, but to march on Philadelphia instead. Another problem was logistical. Dotted by numerous lakes and marked by rivers, upstate New York had impassable swamps and heavy forests with thick undergrowth. There were no real roads, just narrow Indian trails. Colonial axe men felled trees in the British army's path, stalling the soldiers even more. They destroyed bridges and rolled large boulders into fording sites.

There were some bright spots for Burgoyne. He managed to capture Fort Ticonderoga from the Americans, and St. Leger's army captured Fort Schuyler (formerly Fort Stanwix) on August 23. St. Leger had already engaged the Americans in the battle of Oriskany on August 6, in which half the rebel troops were killed or wounded in a single day of fighting.

The Oriskany victory was short-lived. During the battle, Americans had entered the British encampment and looted supplies, including food stocks. St. Leger marched on for a time, until his forces were told by a misinformed Loyalist that a thousands-strong American force under Benedict Arnold was headed their way. The news was enough to make St. Leger's Indian Iroquois allies abandon him; he called off his advance and retreated back west to the relative safety of Fort Niagara. This left General Burgoyne alone in the field to face the Americans.

Burgoyne had already suffered setbacks. On August 16 a group of New Hampshire militia, under the command of General John Stark, defeated a unit of 1,600 Hessians whom Burgoyne had sent out to forage from local farms. During the battle, the German commander, fearing defeat, signaled his drummers to beat for a parley, or peace talks. But the New Hampshire farmers did not understand the drum signal and kept fighting. The Hessians lost, suffering nearly 1,000 casualties.

Soon Burgoyne found his army surrounded by various groups of Continentals and militiamen. The American commander, General Horatio Gates, met the British 30 miles (48 kilometers) outside of Albany. Two battles took place, both near Saratoga, New York, on September 19 and October 7. While Burgoyne's men fought bravely, they were unable to break past the well-entrenched Americans. Burgoyne was defeated and, on October 17, surrendered to General Gates. The great strategy of the "year of the hangman" had failed miserably.

A TURNING POINT

The decisive defeat of the British at Saratoga would have an immediate impact on the war. Most historians consider the American win to symbolize the turning point in the conflict between Great Britain and America. Since the war's beginning, the French had considered siding with the Americans against the British. As long as the Americans appeared to be losing, however, the French king, Louis XVI, had remained

BENEDICT ARNOLD: AMERICAN TRAITOR

Perhaps the most famous traitor in American history is Benedict Arnold, the man who fought gallantly for the Patriots during the early years of the Revolutionary War. Arnold spearheaded the march to Quebec during the first year of the war and was a hero at Saratoga in the fall of 1777. But he turned away from the Patriot cause to help the British later in the war. One of his motivations was his love for a woman.

After Arnold received a serious leg injury during the second Saratoga battle, Washington removed him from field duty, assigning him as military governor of Philadelphia in June 1778 after General Clinton left the city to the rebels. There, he met the beautiful, young Peggy Shippen, with whom he fell in love. Unfortunately, Shippen was loyal to the British.

Slowly, Peggy worked on Arnold, trying to convince him the American cause was lost. Then, American military officials charged Arnold with criminal activities, which led to his conviction of graft and embezzlement. Washington intervened to keep Arnold from being harshly punished, but the incident turned the American war hero against the Patriot cause. Needing money (Peggy demanded a lavish lifestyle), Benedict Arnold cooked up a plan to sell out the Revolution.

After getting himself appointed to command the New York fort at West Point, which controlled the Hudson, Arnold planned to go over to the British side, offering them the plans to West Point so they could capture it. When his plan was discovered, Arnold fled behind British lines. (His accomplice, British Major John Andre, was captured with the West Point plans in his possession and hanged.) Arnold fought for the British for the remainder of the war and died in England.

indecisive. After the Saratoga victory, the French agreed in February 1778 to sign a pair of treaties with the Americans. (Since 1776, American diplomats, including John Adams and Benjamin Franklin, had been in Paris trying to facilitate a French alliance.) The first agreement, the Treaty of Amity (or friendship) and Commerce locked the two nations as trading partners. The second, the Treaty of Friendship and Alliance, called for the two powers to support one another in time of war against Great Britain. The French monarch, of course, had no great love of liberty or independence from royal domination, but he wanted to make things as difficult for the British as possible. In time, the French were sending arms, supplies, food, and even white-uniformed troops to America. Perhaps most importantly, the French navy was now technically at the disposal of the American cause.

While 1777, then, ended as had 1776, with an important American victory, George Washington knew that French support lay in the future. The winter of 1777–1778 was upon his army, which had taken up quarters in Valley Forge, Pennsylvania, named after the iron forges that had been built there years earlier. The encampment was only 20 miles (32 kilometers) from Philadelphia, where a British army would spend a warm winter. In the valley, the Continental army struggled through a season of cold, hunger, and death. Of the 10,000 men camped in the hills and winding hollows of farm country, a quarter of them died. They lived in tents until their huts were constructed. The men ate what they could, often nothing more than doughy cakes made from flour and water. Weather was a constant problem, since blankets, coats, and firewood were not abundant. Shoes were scarce. Disease struck down hundreds.

However, the men spent much of their time in camp drilling, becoming a more-disciplined fighting force. Facing well-trained British armies, it was important that the Americans become accustomed to marching in unison, taking orders during combat, and fighting as an organized force. One of the import drill instructors for the American army was a Prussian volunteer, 50-year-old Friedrich von Steuben. From his experience in the armies of Frederick the Great, von Steuben knew the art of war and how to train soldiers. In earlier battles, American forces had relied on firing their muskets to turn the fight. Von Steuben instructed them in the art of using the bayonet. This was to be a significant change.

ONE MORE NEW JERSEY FIGHT

As British generals and military planners searched for new strategies for 1778, they decided to focus, again, on a region known for higher percentages of Loyalists—the South. Their "Southern Strategy" admitted the new landscape of war. France was soon to become a combatant, and the British knew they would be fighting on more fronts, including the Caribbean and even Europe. British forces would have to be spread around the globe and the possibility of raising massive armies, such as the one that had landed at New York City in 1776, was nearly eliminated. Larger numbers of Loyalists would have to fill the ranks of British resistance to the rebel cause. The British were hoping against hope, however. From the beginning of the war, they had always overestimated the number of Loyalists in America.

In May 1778 the new British strategy was underway. General Henry Clinton had replaced General William Howe. Clinton was a capable leader and had been in the war since Gage's forces had been besieged in Boston. He could not wait to take command and move the war, again, onto southern soil. Before leaving Philadelphia for the South, however, he engaged General Washington in one more fight.

During the summer of 1778, Clinton prepared his troops to leave the Pennsylvania city. His orders from London were

George Washington and Baron von Steuben inspect the colonial army at Valley Forge in February 1778. Von Steuben was a Prussian army general sent by Congress to discipline and train the American troops.

to march from Philadelphia to New York City where 5,000 of his men were to board ships bound for the Caribbean to fight the French. But Clinton was not prepared to give up that many of his troops, so he ignored that part of the order, even as he began marching across New Jersey to New York, a distance of only 70 miles (112 kilometers). Beginning their advance on June 18 after spending two days crossing the Delaware River, the redcoat column, which included 1,500 supply wagons, stretched on for several miles. Camped close by, Washington decided he could not let the British move without attacking. Although his ranks had been decimated by a difficult winter at Valley Forge, spring had brought new recruits. That mid-June, Washington's forces numbered 13,500, with another 2,000 already in New Jersey.

As Clinton's men began their march, Washington's forces pursued them. The American army had drilled heavily that winter, many were seasoned fighters, and they marched, perhaps for the first time, in well-ordered columns. On June 24 Washington met with his officer staff to determine whether to attack Clinton's rear line. Most favored an attack, but on a limited scale. Should the entire British column turn and fight, the Continental army might be annihilated.

The Battle of Monmouth

Two days later, an exhausted British army stumbled into Monmouth, New Jersey. By mid-morning the temperature hit 100 degrees Fahrenheit (38 degrees Centigrade), and men dropped regularly with heat exhaustion. British redcoats, after all, wore heavy woolen uniforms with tight collars, carried 60-lb (27-kg) packs on their backs, along with a musket that weighed 14 lbs (6 kg). At Monmouth, the British line stretched on for 12 miles (19 km) from front to rear. On June 28 Washington made his move. Almost half of Washington's men were thrown into a fight against Clinton's rear line. Early in the fight, however, General Charles Lee, who had been set free by the British and returned to join Washington's army, retreated from the attack, certain his forces were going to be defeated. At that point, little real fighting had even taken place. Lee, who had opposed the attack, had simply failed in his duties.

Washington spurred his horse and moved toward Lee, angrily asking him why he had broken off his attack. Lee seemed confused, and his men were in disarray. He made several excuses, which only angered Washington, who asked him why he had accepted command of the attack if he had not intended to go through with it. On the spot, Washington relieved Lee of his command. It would be his last service under the Virginia general.

Washington had to instantly take Lee's place on the battlefield and rally his men, or the battle would be lost before it had even begun in earnest. For the remainder of the fight, the Americans performed well, revealing their new level of training. (During the battle near Monmouth Courthouse, 37 Americans and 60 redcoats collapsed on the field with sunstroke.) There were casualties on both sides, but the Continental army proved itself that day. It had become a professional fighting force. The battle finally broke off, and Clinton's men marched on to New York City. As for Charles Lee, he was discharged from service in the Continental army.

TAKING THE WAR TO THE SOUTH

Through the following months, Clinton's army was shipped down to southern soil. (Clinton himself did not sail south until late 1779, deciding to remain in the comfort of New York City.) In November 1778 British redcoats captured Savannah, Georgia, and along with it, most of Georgia. Assaults against Charleston, South Carolina, were not as immediately successful. Thousands of Continental troops, along with additional thousands of militia forces, held onto the city through the winter of 1778–1779. From shore batteries, the American fired on British ships in the harbor. When they ran low on cannonballs, they stuffed cannon barrels with everything from large pieces of broken glass to old hatchets and pickaxes. Charleston did not fall until the late spring of 1780. Once that important port was in British hands, General Clinton returned to New York City, never seeing the South again, leaving Charles Cornwallis, a capable, experienced general, in command in the field.

Cornwallis seemed to have plenty of men to carry out the takeover of South Carolina: His army numbered 8,000, and was reinforced by thousands of Loyalists. But he was constantly harassed by small bands of fighters whose hit-and-run raids and ambushes drained his supplies and manpower.

Yet while guerrilla warfare was a constant distraction for Cornwallis and his men, the southern campaign sometimes produced major field battles. To meet the challenge of Cornwallis on southern soil, the Continental Congress had sent General Horatio Gates, the hero of Saratoga, to the Carolinas where he commanded a force of 4,000 men. The first encounter between these two generals took place on the morning of August 16, with Gates's men engaging approximately 2,500 of Cornwallis's troops.

The battle of Camden went miserably for the Americans. Although they outnumbered Cornwallis's army, many of Gates's soldiers were untrained and untested. In addition, many were ill, so that perhaps half of the American army was ineffective in the fight. At the first British attack, the Continentals simply fell apart. Gates galloped away from the battlefield altogether, surfacing in Charlotte, North Carolina, some 60 miles (100 kilometers) away. Washington quickly replaced Gates with another commander, the effective and skilled Nathaniel Greene. Washington was eager to make the replacement. He and Gates had experienced a falling out following Gates's victory at Saratoga in October 1777. Gates had engaged in a conspiracy with another general, Thomas Conway, along with several congressmen to replace Washington with Gates. Washington and other loyal congressmen discovered the plot, which was quickly exposed, yet Gates retained his command—at least until the days following his humiliating loss at Camden.

KINGS MOUNTAIN AND THE COWPENS

In October, a portion of Cornwallis's army engaged American frontiersmen known as the "Over the Mountain" men, who thought the British were bringing the war too close to them. On October 7, 1,100 troops, mostly Loyalists, fought these backwoodsmen along the South Carolina/North Carolina border at a site called Kings Mountain. The British commander in the battle, Major Patrick Ferguson, was killed, and most of his army destroyed. After the fight, the frontiersmen took nine Loyalists and hanged them.

With the loss of Ferguson and his men, Cornwallis's long-range left flank had been destroyed, leaving his main army more vulnerable. Guerrilla forces continued to be a problem and now General Greene sought a battle with the British general. Greene had split his forces into two separately moving armies, one of which engaged British troops on January 17, 1781 in a fight 100 miles (160 km) southwest of Kings Mountain, in a rolling meadow called the Cowpens. Here, the American commander, a rough-and-tumble brigadier general named Daniel Morgan, engaged redcoats and Loyalists under a British cavalry officer, Banastre Tarleton, who was thoroughly despised in the southern states.

Morgan quickly gained the upper hand. After only one hour of fighting, Tarleton lost nearly 1,000 men, including 100 killed. Morgan had only lost 70 men. The day ended in a lopsided defeat for the British. Uncertain what other British armies he might have to face, Morgan soon reattached his remaining 500 men to General Greene's main force.

In March 1781 Greene and Cornwallis again met on the battlefield, this time at Guilford Courthouse in central North Carolina. Outnumbered two to one, Greene's men were outfought, but Cornwallis suffered high casualties. There appeared to be no end in sight for Cornwallis and his men, who were dwindling in number. Although Clinton had ordered him not to march his army north to Virginia, Cornwallis felt he had no other option. Loyalists were too few in number to supplement his forces, and the Carolinas had proven a hotbed of opposition. He turned southeast and marched his forces to Wilmington, North Carolina, and from there, continued north toward Virginia, finally reaching a tiny tobacco port called Yorktown.

SHOWDOWN AT YORKTOWN

When General Clinton received the news that Cornwallis had moved his army into Virginia, he was furious. He thought his colleague had given up on the southern campaign too soon. To make certain Cornwallis did not get caught unexpectedly by the enemy, he ordered him to place his forces in defenses around Yorktown.

Not only did word reach Clinton of Cornwallis's march to Virginia; General Washington received the same intelligence. It was now six years since the battles of Lexington and Concord. In May French troops arrived, under the command of the Comte de Rochambeau. Washington's first plan was to march on New York and remove the British presence there, but Rochambeau suggested that the Americans march instead on Virginia and corner Cornwallis's army. If Cornwallis's forces could be trapped and defeated, Washington might pull off a great victory. Washington agreed.

Rochambeau had already ordered French Admiral de Grasse and his fleet to Chesapeake Bay to block the British navy from evacuating Cornwallis and his men from the Yorktown peninsula. In the first week of July, French troops joined Washington's army. The well-disciplined French soldiers, in their smart white uniforms, made the Continental army look a bit shabby and unprofessional. But one French officer would later write, according to historian Middlekauff: "It is incredible that soldiers composed of whites and blacks, almost naked, unpaid, and rather poorly fed, can march so well and stand fire so steadfastly." ✳

The French Provide Support

In September Washington and his main force joined their comrades in Virginia. Clinton had ordered British troops to keep a watchful eye on Washington's encampments north

BATTLES OF THE REVOLUTIONARY WAR

The American Revolutionary War—also known as the American War of Independence—lasted from April 1775 to October 1781. More than 25,000 American and 20,000 British soldiers were killed or died of wounds or disease. Britain was defeated by the Americans, fighting for their freedom and their homes, and helped by the French.

Sites of significant battles in the Revolutionary War.

THE BATTLE AT YORKTOWN, VIRGINIA, 1781

Washington's forces strengthened their position by digging trenches, erecting defenses, and then bringing in heavy guns. Their mortar and cannon fire was devastatingly accurate. British resistance was weak as redcoats became unnerved by the thundering of the cannon and the distressing cries of their wounded.

For six days, allied forces kept up an artillery barrage against the British positions.

Not long after the battle, Marquis de Lafayette, an aide to Washington who had monitored and helped stall Cornwallis's movements in the build-up to the confrontation, wrote home to France. "Here," he said, "humanity has won its battle, liberty now has a country."

of New York. But the wily American general had left with most of his men under cover of darkness, leaving behind a skeleton force that kept a large number of campfires burning each night so the British would think there were more of them still north of the city than there actually were. By the time Clinton realized he had been fooled, the Continental army was long gone, leaving him with few options. At the same time, the French arrived in Chesapeake Bay with 27 ships, 74 cannon, and 3,000 new French troops. When Clinton sent a few ships south to rescue Cornwallis on the Virginia peninsula, they were turned around by de Grasse's superior force.

Washington and Rochambeau Plan the Attack

Every element was in place for Washington to launch a full-scale attack against Cornwallis's army. As noted by historian Alan Axelrod, Cornwallis sent a dispatch to General Clinton on September 23, telling him: "If you cannot relieve me very soon, you must be prepared to hear the worst."

Washington, now back in Virginia and still commanding men in the field, knew the battle facing him was his to lose. His forces, which already greatly outnumbered those of Cornwallis, reached a total of 16,000 once de Grasse landed another 3,000 support troops. But the clock was ticking down. De Grasse's fleet was scheduled to sail out on October 15. Washington and Rochambeau, meeting on de Grasse's grand flagship, worked out a hurried plan to lay siege to Cornwallis's positions. With the French navy continuing to block Chesapeake Bay, Washington and Rochambeau's men would bombard British positions, as allied engineers dug zigzag siege trenches to allow the armies to move in closer. On October 1 Washington ordered an artillery barrage that continued for the next six days. Gunners were so accurate in their shelling that they were able to bombard the last two

A British officer, on behalf of General Charles Cornwallis, surrenders to American General George Washington at Yorktown, Virginia, ending the fighting in the American Revolutionary War on October 19, 1781.

remaining British frigates supporting Cornwallis out of the York River. Then, on October 6, the engineers began digging their approach trenches.

The British Surrender

On October 14 a French officer, along with an American aide to Washington, Alexander Hamilton, led a nighttime bayonet charge against two British redoubts, or defensive forts, near the York River. This left Cornwallis extremely vulnerable to large-scale attack and also allowed the trench excavations to extend all the way to the river. Cornwallis's time was up. There was no possible escape. At 10 A.M. on October 17 a British drummer mounted a parapet and beat a parley, signaling to the French and Americans that Cornwallis was ready to talk surrender terms. Before the day was over, General Cornwallis agreed to Washington's terms—unaware that General Clinton had sent out a rescue mission from New York that same day. Two days later Clinton received word of Cornwallis's surrender and turned around, returning to New York City.

On October 19 the American Revolutionary War technically ended. Cornwallis surrendered on the field of battle, and no major battles took place during the months and years that followed. The British still held onto such cities as New York, Charleston, and Savannah, and limited fighting took place here and there, primarily between Loyalists and Patriots in the South. On March 4, 1782, members of the British Parliament voted to abandon the fight. After nearly seven years of difficult war, the Americans had finally gained from Great Britain the one objective they had fixed in their hearts and minds—independence.

8

A New Form of Government

Washington's victory at Yorktown was the last major battle of the American Revolutionary War. In March 1782 the British ministry, which had been led by Lord Frederick North since 1770, collapsed. The new government established peace talks with American representatives, including John Adams, John Jay, and Benjamin Franklin. (Jay would later become America's first chief justice of the Supreme Court.)

These skillful men knew how to negotiate the best terms possible, and the resulting Treaty of Paris, signed on September 3, 1783, could not have been more favorable to America. Independence was recognized. Britain surrendered all claims to territory between the Atlantic Coast and the Mississippi River, a vast piece of land. The boundary from north to south ran from the Great Lakes to Spanish-controlled Florida. In addition, John Adams managed to get the British to give American fishermen unlimited fishing rights off the coast of Newfoundland, a minor concession in the larger picture, but important to his fellow New Englanders.

THE ARTICLES OF CONFEDERATION

More than 20 years had passed since the end of the French and Indian War. During those two decades the 13 colonies had defied the Crown, which led to a rebellion, which caused a war, that created a separate nation—the United States of America. Even while the American Revolutionary War was taking place, the Second Continental Congress had created a new country, a confederation of 13 states based on representative government and a written constitution. That first constitution—the Articles of Confederation—was adopted by Congress in 1777, but the document was not ratified, or approved by the states, until 1781.

That constitution established the distribution of power between the states and the national government, with the states holding much of that power, and the national government being fairly weak. In its details, much of that national government was very different to the national government of today. That early government consisted almost entirely of a unicameral, or one-house, legislature. There was no president or vice president or even an executive branch. There was no national court system, or judiciary. For some of the Patriot leaders, such as Samuel Adams or Thomas Paine, this was an ideal system: no single strong government wielding too much power at the expense of the various states. Others, such as John Adams, thought the arrangement too loose, lacking a head, and "too democratical." Adams's concern was that there was no government branch or structure to balance the power of the one-house congress.

There were significant other issues with the Articles of Confederation government. The constitution provided no power for the national government to tax. It could ask the states for money, but they did not have to pay if they chose not to. As a result, throughout the 1780s states typically sent only about half the monies requested. The national government had no power to regulate trade between the states either, as that power was held by the states.

From New England to Georgia, many American people began to see their national government as too weak, especially to be able to solve any significant financial or economic problems. When the Articles of Confederation Congress needed money, it just printed more, to the tune of $220 mil-

ORGANIZING THE WEST

The Treaty of Paris (September 1783) not only recognized independence for the new United States, it also set the young nation's new boundaries. The country included the lands stretching from the Great Lakes in the north to the Gulf of Mexico, minus Florida. It spanned the territory from the Atlantic Coast to the Mississippi. Much of this land lay west of the Appalachian Mountains, and few Americans lived there. But more were moving west following the Revolutionary War, as veterans received land grants for their war service. The Articles of Confederation government recognized that these western lands needed to be organized.

While the Articles government failed in many ways, one of its successful legacies was the passing of laws, called ordinances, that helped set up government in the west and to survey the land so that new residents could gain legal title. The first was the Ordinance of 1784, which was first proposed by Thomas Jefferson. It called for the dividing of the lands north of the Ohio River (known as the Northwest Territory) into ten future states and a survey to establish blocks of land called townships, each 10 miles (16 km) square. It also guaranteed all new states the right to self-government.

The following year, the national government passed the Ordinance

lion in paper currency, with no backing in gold or silver. Veterans of the Revolutionary War, who had fought for independence, could not be paid. By 1783 the country was on the verge of a great economic depression. Even the weather did not cooperate, as farmers experienced two bad harvests in a row for the years 1784 and 1785. Great Britain only made things worse. Even though the war was over, the British authorities tried to hamper the development and stability of the young United States. Parliament cut off the sale of American goods in the British West Indies. As the post-war

of 1785, which altered the previous ordinance. It changed the number of future states from ten to between three and five (the Northwest Territory would eventually be carved up into five states: Ohio, Indiana, Illinois, Michigan, and Wisconsin). The townships were changed into blocks of land measuring six square miles (9.6 square km), making a total of 36 squares of land each measuring one square mile (1.6 square km), or 640 acres (260 hectares). Land in these townships would be sold as square miles of property, no less. The price was set at $1 per acre (0.4 hectares), totaling $640 per section of a township.

In 1787 a third land act, the Northwest Ordinance, passed through the Congress. This law established a three-step procedure by which a territory could become a state. First, Congress was to appoint officials for a given territory to serve as the territorial government. Then, when the number of free male landowners of voting age reached 5,000, the territory could elect its own legislature and send a nonvoting delegate to Congress. Last, when the territory's population reached 60,000 (the population of the smallest state in the Union), residents could write a state constitution and apply to Congress for statehood.

These laws, especially those passed in 1785 and 1787, cleared the way for creating new states, making them some of the most important legislation created by the Articles of Confederation government.

economy spiraled downward, some Americans took events into their own hands.

SHAYS'S REBELLION

Many of those Americans hit hard by bad economic times and poor harvests were farmers. In western Massachusetts, times proved extremely difficult. A large number of farmers were deeply in debt with land mortgages and other loans. Those who could not pay their debts faced foreclosure and the possible loss of their lands and livelihood. Many farmers hoped the Massachusetts legislature might pass "stay laws"—designed to limit a creditor's ability to take someone's land for non-payment of debts—but not only did the legislature not pass such laws, it even approved higher taxes. When farmers protested, state lawmakers simply turned a blind eye. By mid-decade hundreds of Massachusetts farmers were prepared to take up arms in protest.

One of the early leaders of this dissatisfied movement was a 39-year-old veteran of the battle of Breed's Hill, Daniel Shays. In 1786 a group of his followers, soon referred to as Shays's Rebels, raided local courts to stop farm foreclosures and broke into jails to free farmers who had been arrested for nonpayment of debts. Other farmers, inspired by their efforts, joined Shays's Rebellion. At one point the Massachusetts government called out the state militia to put down the uprising. In January 1787, following an attack by disgruntled farmers on the federal arsenal in Springfield, 600 militia met more than 1,000 rebellious farmers, some of whom were armed only with pitchforks. The militia dispersed them with cannon fire. Four fell dead, another 20 were wounded, and the others scattered. After another force of some 4,000 militia attacked a group of rebels in the village of Petersham, the movement collapsed, and Shays barely escaped. To help defuse the rebellion, the state legislature lowered taxes and offered amnesty to all those who had participated in the civil disobedience.

Yet Shays's Rebellion was worrisome to many in America, especially those who believed the Articles of Confederation were partly to blame. George Washington himself, then in retirement at his home in Mount Vernon, Virginia, was aghast at the violence that spread across Massachusetts, stating, as noted by historian John Ferling: "Good God! There are combustibles in every State, which a spark may set fire to." Washington feared the British would take "every opportunity to foment [stir up] the spirit of turbulence within the bowels of the United States." He and others believed that the Articles should be amended to create a stronger national government, one that could function properly so that such uprisings did not become commonplace.

A CONVENTION IN PHILADELPHIA

In the four years following the Treaty of Paris, a significant number of Americans became dissatisfied with their national government's inability to handle both domestic and foreign problems. To many, the country seemed on the verge of chaos. The leaders of other governments, especially in Europe, viewed the young nation with skepticism, not sure whether the great American experiment in liberty would succeed.

The Articles of Confederation seemed to represent the primary problem for the new nation. Its framers had spread out power between the states at the expense of the national government and that system based on confederation—what the Articles referred to as, recalled by historian Catherine Drinker Bowen, a "firm league of friendship"—had proven unworkable. By 1787 the American discontent had reached its zenith.

Even the previous year, James Madison, a member of the Virginia assembly, had proposed a national convention in which the states could discuss problems with trade between one another. Five states had sent delegates to that convention, held in Annapolis, Maryland. It was during those sit-downs that some of the delegates suggested a follow-up meeting for the next summer to be held in Philadelphia to, as noted by historian Gordon S. Wood, "devise such further provisions as shall appear . . . necessary to render the Constitution of the Federal Government adequate to the exigencies of the Union." In short, they wanted to meet to discuss fixing the structural problems in the Articles of Confederation.

Over several weeks in May 1787 delegates straggled into Philadelphia where they spent a long hot summer thrash-

A SECRET CONVENTION

From the first meeting of the Philadelphia Convention, the delegates almost unanimously chose to carry out their business completely in secret. Since many had been chosen for the purpose of amending or changing the Articles of Confederation, their decision to scrap the Articles was one the people might not approve.

Also, if the public knew the delegates were writing a new constitution, there might be pressure put on them to make certain decisions or avoid difficult debates. Without worrying about popular opinion or public opposition, the delegates were free to hammer their way through the creation of a completely new framework of government.

While nearly every member of the Convention was able to keep the direction and content of meetings secret, one delegate, it seems, could not—the elderly Benjamin Franklin. During dinner parties, Franklin had a habit of talking too much and telling about a given day's proceedings. This led his fellow delegates to assign someone to accompany Franklin at such gatherings, someone who could steer dinner conversations away from the delicate work of the Convention.

ing through potential changes to the Articles of Confederation—until they determined to scrap the whole document
and start over again with an entirely new constitution. Sev-
enty-four men were chosen as delegates to the Philadelphia
convention. Fifty-five delegates showed up. Many of them
were young men, with more of them under the age of 30
than were over the age of 60. They were businessmen, diplomats, legislators, war leaders, and lawyers—many lawyers. They had graduated from various colleges, many were
wealthy, and all felt they had serious stakes in the future of
the American republic. Three out of four had served in the
Continental Congress. Eight had signed the Declaration of
Independence. Seven had been state governors. Many had
participated in writing their state constitutions. About one
out of three owned slaves.

Madison Gets to Work

Several of the Philadelphia Convention delegates were
among the Founding Fathers—Alexander Hamilton, James
Madison, Benjamin Franklin (the eldest man attending),
and George Washington, who was chosen as the president
of the convention. Others who had struggled to make the
break with Great Britain, including Samuel Adams and Patrick Henry, were not present. John Adams was in London
and Thomas Jefferson in Paris, both working on trade treaties on behalf of the United States. Thomas Paine, the writer
of *Common Sense* and other influential revolutionary pamphlets—together often known as *The American Crisis*—had
gone back to England to find backers willing to invest in his
new invention, a type of iron bridge.

None had prepared for the political work that summer
more than James Madison from Virginia, who had purchased
and read more than 200 books on everything from political
government to economics to Greek and Roman histories.

Slowly, but deliberately, the delegates began considering the various problems of the Articles of Confederation. Five issues bubbled to the surface: 1) the government's absolute financial chaos; 2) the government's inability to control trade, as the Articles allowed each state to make its own commercial treaties with foreign powers; 3) the lack of political stability, leaving the nation vulnerable to the advantage of the British and the Spanish, for example; 4) endless arguments

George Washington (standing on the right) presides at the Constitutional Convention in the Old State House, or Independence Hall, in Philadelphia in July 1787. This painting of 1856 is by American artist Junius Brutus Stearns.

between states over such issues as trade and even state borders; and 5) the lack of street-level democracy, including limits on who could vote and a lack of elections.

Most of the delegates were in agreement that a basic problem with the Articles was that it framed a government that rested on only one branch—the legislative. Several plans were proposed to deal with that issue. Madison himself presented a proposal that became known as the Virginia Plan, in which he suggested three branches of government: legislative (to make laws), executive (to enforce laws), and judicial (courts to interpret laws). His plan also called for a two-house congress, with membership of both houses based on the population of each state.

Establishing a Solution

An immediate block went up on the part of several smaller states, their delegates feeling that Madison's system would favor larger, more populous states, such as his Virginia or Hamilton's New York. A delegate named William Paterson proposed an alternative called the New Jersey Plan, which suggested a unicameral legislature with equal representation per state regardless of anything, including population. It also provided for a chief executive to enforce the laws and a Supreme Court. The suggestion of a unicameral legislature with equal representation was completely unacceptable to the larger states. It would allow, for example, Rhode Island (whose population was 68,000) as much representative power as Virginia (whose population was 747,000). For the New Jersey Plan's critics, this translated into power kept in the hands of the states, rather than the people.

For weeks, the delegates argued over the two plans, coming nowhere close to an agreement. Then, on July 2, 11 years to the day since the Second Continental Congress had voted in favor of independence from Great Britain, the delegates proposed a committee to try to settle the issue. That committee produced an agreement that became known as the Great Compromise. It called for a House of Representatives, with membership based on a state's population: the more people, the more representatives. It also set up a Senate, with equal representation, based on two senators per state. To give the House an extra layer of power, it was decided that all money or tax bills would originate in the House.

More controversy was generated. Southerners wanted to count their large slave populations for determining the number of their representatives, even though black slaves would not be allowed to vote nor would they be counted as citizens. Again, a compromise was made, allowing southerners to count each slave as three-fifths (60 percent) of a person for representation. However, they had to count them by the same ratio for the purpose of taxation.

Another argument developed over slavery which threatened to block any more progress in the convention. Some northerners wanted to see the slave trade ended on American soil, a move the southern delegates could not agree to. Again, compromise broke the impasse. Southerners were assured that the new U.S. Congress would not enact laws limiting the slave trade for at least 20 years, until 1808. Also, all later changes made by Congress concerning trade laws would require a two-thirds majority. The compromise did not make everyone happy, including some southerners. According to historian John Ferling, Virginian James Madison, who owned slaves, wrote: "Great as the evil is, a dismemberment of the Union would be worse."

A NEW CONSTITUTION

On July 26 a new committee was established, the Committee of Detail, to write the new constitution. During their work, the committee members decided that the new chief executive, who was to be called "president," would be chosen by an electoral college of men selected by local voters. Additional compromises and decisions had to be made, as well, but the new document was ready for a vote by September. On September 17, 39 delegates accepted and signed the United States Constitution. Some had already left for home and were not present. A handful of delegates refused to sign the document, feeling a bill of rights should have been included to protect each individual's rights. Such an addition was made before the Constitution was ratified by the states on June 2, 1788.

A great sea change had taken place as the people of the United States rejected their first national framework of government in favor of another. The new Constitution represented more power in the hands of the people. That very point is acknowledged in the document's opening paragraph, or preamble, which opens with the words: "We the People, to form a more perfect Union . . ."

Setting the Scene

With the establishment of a new Constitution, the United States would enter an era of unparalleled redefining of government. No longer would national power rest in a single house legislature, one hamstrung by the power of the states. The political will of the people would be distributed as never before, through the Constitution's three branches, including an executive embodied in the office of the president. Those men of America's future, those first chief executives—including such Founding Fathers as Washington, Adams, and Jefferson—would chart new directions for their country, including one that would soon expand westward, stretching the influence of the new American republic beyond the Appalachians toward the heart of the North American continent.

Chronology

1755–62 Britain wins the French and Indian War, but emerges from the war deeply in debt

1763 Pontiac's War results in the deaths of 2,000 English colonists. The Crown sends more British soldiers to the American colonies and restricts the movement of colonists west of the Appalachians.

1764 British prime minister Lord Grenville pushes the Sugar Act through Parliament, establishing trade

TIMELINE

1764
British prime minister Lord Grenville pushes the Sugar Act through Parliament

1765
March. Parliament passes the Stamp Act

1770
Rioting in Boston results in the "Boston Massacre"

1755   1759   1763   1767   1771

1766
Parliament repeals the Stamp Act

1767
Parliament passes the Townshend Duties

duties on foreign goods commonly imported into the American colonies

1765

March Parliament passes the revenue-generating Stamp Act, creating new taxes on the American colonies

June James Otis prompts the Massachusetts General Court to propose an intercolonial meeting to protest the Stamp Act

August 14 Boston protesters ransack a stamp agent's home

October 31 New York merchants suggest a boycott of British goods as a means of protesting against the Stamp Act

1773
December 16. Boston Tea Party

1774
September. Twelve colonies send 56 delegates to the First Continental Congress

1777
American General Horatio Gates defeats General Johnny Burgoyne in the battle of Saratoga

1788
The new U.S. Constitution is ratified

1787
Constitutional convention at Philadelphia. Northwest Ordinance is passed

1772   **1776**   **1780**   **1784**   **1788**

1775
April 19. British and American troops fire on one another on the green at Lexington and on the bridge outside Concord
June 17. British and colonists fight the battle of Breed's Hill or Bunker Hill

1776
July 4. Congress votes to accept the Declaration of Independence.
December. Washington wins strategic victory

1781
Washington defeats General Cornwallis's army near Yorktown

1775
June 17. British and colonists fight the battle of Breed's Hill

1766 Parliament repeals the Stamp Act in March, but also passes the Declaratory Act, proclaiming Parliament's power to pass any law it wishes governing the colonies

1767 Parliament passes the Townshend Duties on a list of trade commodities to the colonies, including tea

1770 Rioting in Boston results in British troops killing five protesters—the "Boston Massacre"

1772

June Rhode Island residents board and set alight an armed British customs schooner, the *Gaspée*

November Patriots attending a Boston town meeting create the first Committee of Correspondence

1773

September East India Company delivers 600,000 pounds (272,155 kilograms) of tea to American cities under the Tea Act and the Townshend Duties

November 28 Three tea ships arrive in Boston Harbor, where locals stop the cargo being offloaded

December 16 About 60 colonials dressed as Mohawk Indians board the tea ships and throw the tea overboard, remembered as the Boston Tea Party

1774

September Twelve colonies send 56 delegates to the meeting known as the First Continental Congress

October As the First Continental Congress adjourns, the delegates pass the Declaration and Resolves of the Continental Congress, declaring Parliament's restricted legislative power over the colonies

1775

January 27 Lord Dartmouth, the king's representative in the colonies, sends orders to General Gage to round up colonial agitators Sam Adams and John Hancock

April 18 British troops march out of Boston to round up revolutionary leaders and take Patriot weapons

April 19 British and American troops fire on one another at Lexington and Concord. The shooting war of the American Revolution opens

June 15 Congress selects George Washington to lead the Continental army

June 17 British and colonists fight the battle of Breed's Hill

1776

January Thomas Paine publishes *Common Sense*

May 10 Congress accepts John Adams's resolution for each colony to set up new constitutional governments

June 7 Richard Henry Lee presents a resolution to Congress, calling for independence for the newly formed states

June 9 Congress forms a five-man committee to draft a declaration of independence

July 2 Congress votes to accept the Lee resolution, making the colonies "free and independent states"

July 4 Congress votes to accept the Declaration of Independence

1777 Americans win the battle of Saratoga, encouraging the French to enter the Revolution as allies

1778 American seaport of Savannah falls to the British

1780 American seaport of Charleston falls to the British

1781 Washington defeats Cornwallis's army near Yorktown on October 19, ending the Revolutionary War

1785 Land Ordinance of 1785

1786 Shays's Rebellion

1787 Constitutional convention at Philadelphia. Northwest Ordinance is passed

1788 The new U.S. Constitution is ratified

Glossary

actual representation The political theory that people must participate in the selection of those who serve as their representatives, through nominating or electing.

boycott The collective refusal by a group of people to participate in a given activity.

constitution A written framework of laws that sets out the rights of the people, the power of the government, and the government's structure.

Crown British power embodied in the monarchy (the king or queen) and Parliament.

customs duties Payments made on imports for the purpose of regulating trade.

Founding Fathers The term used by historians to refer to those who played key roles in the American Revolution and the establishment of the United States of America as a new nation.

impressment A common practice of the British navy during the eighteenth and nineteenth centuries that involved the forced recruitment (often through kidnapping) of sailors into service in the British navy.

Loyalist A British subject living in America who remained loyal to the British government during the American Revolution.

militia Citizens who volunteered to be part-time soldiers.

parley A European custom of combat that may be called by participants on either side for the purpose of negotiating a conclusion of the conflict, such as surrender terms.

Parliament The law-making body of Great Britain.

Patriot An American who wanted the colonies to be free from Britain. About one-third of colonists were Patriots.

redoubt An earthen fort or breastworks designed for defense and to fortify a portion of a larger field of battle.

stay laws Laws for the purpose of limiting one's ability to foreclosure on another due to nonpayment of debts or a mortgage.

Tidewater Refers to the region of the Chesapeake, which includes Maryland and Virginia.

unicameral A single-house legislature.

virtual representation The political theory that people may be represented by a power base even when they did not directly elect or choose those holding power over them.

volley To fire a line of muskets in unison.

Bibliography

Axelrod, Alan. *The Real History of the American Revolution: A New Look at the Past.* New York: Sterling Publishing, 2007.

Boatner, Mark M. *Encyclopedia of the American Revolution.* New York: D. McKay Co, 1974.

Bowen, Catherine Drinker. *Miracle at Philadelphia: The Story of the Constitutional Convention, May to September 1787.* Boston: Little, Brown and Company. An Atlantic Monthly Press Book, 1966.

Boyer, Paul S. *The Enduring Vision: A History of the American People.* Lexington, MA: Houghton Mifflin Company, 2000.

Carey, George. *The Political Writings of John Adams.* Washington, D.C.: Regnery Gateway, 2000.

Ellis, Joseph J. *His Excellency, George Washington.* New York: Alfred A. Knopf, 2004.

Ferling, John. *A Leap in the Dark: The Struggle to Create the American Republic.* New York: Oxford University Press, 2003.

Flexner, James Thomas. *Washington: The Indispensable Man.* Boston: Little, Brown and Company, 1974.

Higginbotham, Don. *The War of American Independence: Military Attitudes, Policies, and Practice, 1763–1789.* New York: Macmillan, 1971.

Jensen, Merrill. *The Articles of Confederation.* Madison, WI: University of Wisconsin Press, 1970.

Lancaster, Bruce. *History of the American Revolution.* New York: Simon & Schuster, Inc., 2003.

Leckie, Robert. *George Washington's War: The Saga of the American Revolution.* New York: Harper Perennial, 1992.

Martin, James Kirby. *America and Its People.* New York: HarperCollins, 1993.

McCullough, David. *John Adams*. New York: Simon & Schuster, 2001.

——. *1776*. New York: Simon & Schuster, 2005.

Middlekauff, Robert. *The Glorious Cause: The American Revolution, 1763–1789*. New York: Oxford University Press, 2005.

Morris, Richard B. *The Forging of the Union, 1781–1789*. New York: Harper & Row, 1987.

Purcell, L. Edward, and David F. Burg. *The World Almanac of the American Revolution*. New York: World Almanac, 1992.

Rhodehamel, John. *The American Revolution: Writings from the War of Independence*. Library of America. New York: Literary Classics of the United States, 2001.

Stokesbury, James L. *A Short History of the American Revolution*. New York: William Morrow, 1991.

Unger Harlow. *John Hancock, Merchant King and American Patriot*. Hoboken, NJ: John Wiley & Sons, 2000.

Weinstein, Allen, and Frank Otto Gatell. *Freedom and Crisis: An American History*. New York: Random House, 1981.

Weisberger, Bernard, *The Story of America*. Pleasantville, NY: Reader's Digest Association, Inc., 1975.

Wells, William V. *The Life and Public Services of Samuel Adams*. Boston: Little, Brown and Company, 1865.

Wood, Gordon S. *The Creation of the American Republic, 1776–1787*. Chapel Hill, NC: University of North Carolina Press, 1969.

Further Resources

Bliven, Bruce, Jr. *The American Revolution.* New York: Random House Children's Books, 1981.

Cheney, Lynne. *We the People: The Story of Our Constitution.* New York: Simon & Schuster Children's Publishing, 2008.

————. *When Washington Crossed the Delaware: A Wintertime Story for Young Patriots.* New York: Simon & Schuster Adult Publishing Group, 2004.

DeFord, Deborah H. *American Revolution.* Strongsville, OH: Gareth Stevens Publishing, 2006.

Farshtey, Greg T. *American Revolution.* San Diego: Gale Group, 2003.

Fradin, Dennis Brindell. *Let It Begin Here!: Lexington and Concord: First Battles of the American Revolution.* New York: Walker & Company, 2005.

Herbert, Janis. *The American Revolution for Kids.* Chicago: Chicago Review Press, Inc., 2002.

Maestro, Betsy. *Liberty or Death: The American Revolution: 1763–1783.* New York: HarperCollins Children's Books, 2005.

Murray, Stuart. *American Revolution.* New York: DK Publishing, Inc., 2005.

Nardo, Don. *American Revolution.* San Diego: Gale Group, 2001.

Reit, Seymour V. *Guns for General Washington: A Story of the American Revolution.* New York: Harcourt Children's Books, 2001.

Schanzer, Rosalyn. *George vs. George: The American Revolution as Seen from Both Sides.* Washington, DC: National Geographic Society Children's Books, 2007.

Web sites

American Revolution.com: http://www.americanrevolution.com

Boston Tea Party Ships and Museum: http://www.
bostonteapartyship.com

HistoryCentral.com—Revolutionary War: http://www.
historycentral.com/revolt

Library of Congress—Declaring Independence:
http://www.lcweb.loc.gov/exhibits/declara/declara1.html

National Museum of American History: http://www.
americanhistory.si.edu

National Park Service—Valley Forge: http://www.nps.gov/vafo

National Parks Service Museum Collections—American Revolution:
http://www.nps.gov/history/museum/exhibits/revwar

Old North Church, Boston: http://www.oldnorth.com

Public Broadcasting Service: Liberty! The American Revolution:
http://www.pbs.org/ktca/liberty/

Social Studies for Kids—The American Revolutionary War:
http://www.socialstudiesforkids.com/subjects/
revolutionarywar.htm

The American Revolutionary War: http://myrevolutionarywar.com

The Freedom Trail Foundation: http://www.thefreedomtrail.org

The Paul Revere House: http://www.paulreverehouse.org

USHistory.org—The Declaration of Independence:
http://www.ushistory.org/March/timeline.htm

Yorktown Victory Center: http://www.historyisfun.org/yorktown/
yorktown.cfm

Picture Credits

Page

Index

About the Author

Tim McNeese is associate professor of history at York College in York, Nebraska. Professor McNeese holds degrees from York College, Harding University, and Missouri State University. He has published more than 100 books and educational materials. His writing has earned him a citation in the library reference work, *Contemporary Authors* and multiple citations in *Best Books for Young Teen Readers*. In 2006, Tim appeared on the History Channel program, *Risk Takers, History Makers: John Wesley Powell and the Grand Canyon*. He was been a faculty member at the Tony Hillerman Writers Conference in Albuquerque. His wife, Beverly, is assistant professor of English at York College. They have two married children, Noah and Summer, and three grandchildren—Ethan, Adrianna, and Finn William. Tim and Bev have sponsored college study trips on the Lewis and Clark Trail and to the American Southwest. You may contact Professor McNeese at tdmcneese@york.edu

About the Consultant

Richard Jensen is Research Professor at Montana State University, Billings. He has published 11 books on a wide range of topics in American political, social, military, and economic history, as well as computer methods. After taking a Ph.D. at Yale in 1966, he taught at numerous universities, including Washington, Michigan, Harvard, Illinois-Chicago, West Point, and Moscow State University in Russia.